Jumpin' JUMBLE®

Nimble Puzzles for Active Minds

Henri Arnold, Bob Lee,
and Mike Argirion

TRIUMPH
B O O K S

This book is available in quantity at special discounts
for your group or organization.

For further information, contact:

Triumph Books
814 North Franklin Street
Chicago, Illinois 60610
(312) 939-3330

Printed in U.S.A.

ISBN: 978-1-60078-027-1

Design by Sue Knopf

CONTENTS

Jumpin'
JUMBLE®

Classic Puzzles

JUMBLE®

Unscramble these four Jumbles, one letter to each square, to form four ordinary words.

IKYTT

LAVEE

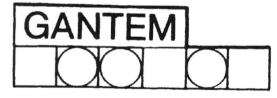

KABREY

GANTEM

WHERE THE OPERA SINGER'S LITTLE ARIA CAME FROM.

Now arrange the circled letters to form the surprise answer, as suggested by the above cartoon.

Print answer here

JUMBLE®

Unscramble these four Jumbles, one letter to each square, to form four ordinary words.

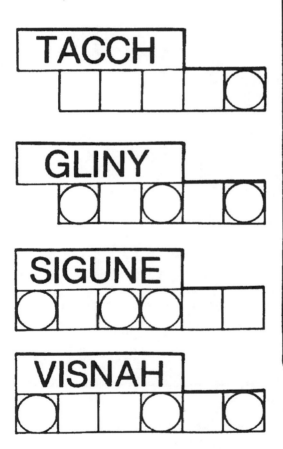

TACCH

GLINY

SIGUNE

VISNAH

WHAT THERE WAS PLENTY OF AT THAT PENTHOUSE.

Now arrange the circled letters to form the surprise answer, as suggested by the above cartoon.

Print answer here

JUMBLE®

Unscramble these four Jumbles, one letter to each square, to form four ordinary words.

GEWIH

NUBEG

TYLPEN

AURBUE
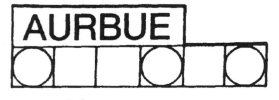

Boy—are you fat!

HOW SOME FRANK PEOPLE MAKE THEIR POINT.

Now arrange the circled letters to form the surprise answer, as suggested by the above cartoon.

Print answer here BY

JUMBLE ®

Unscramble these four Jumbles, one letter to each square, to form four ordinary words.

BUTOD

KWONN

TEECIX

JAVILO

WHAT THE BUS DRIVER SAID.

Now arrange the circled letters to form the surprise answer, as suggested by the above cartoon.

Print answer here " ⎔⎔⎔⎔ ," IN THE ⎔⎔⎔ !

JUMBLE

Unscramble these four Jumbles, one letter to each square, to form four ordinary words.

MEWNO

ENPAC

DEVAHL

TRUGET

WHAT THOSE TALKATIVE MOTHS DID.

Now arrange the circled letters to form the surprise answer, as suggested by the above cartoon.

Print answer here ◯◯◯◯◯◯ THE ◯◯◯

JUMBLE®

Unscramble these four Jumbles, one letter to each square, to form four ordinary words.

NAIRY

BUICT

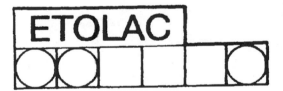

ETOLAC

DULBOY

TIRED OF LOOKING AT ALL THOSE ROADSIDE ADS.

Now arrange the circled letters to form the surprise answer, as suggested by the above cartoon.

Print answer here " ⬡⬡⬡⬡ – ⬡⬡⬡⬡⬡ "

JUMBLE®

Unscramble these four Jumbles, one letter to
each square, to form four ordinary words.

AKARP

CITOX

DYPSOR

CRADOC

WHAT A PERSON
WHO SPENDS
EVERY AFTERNOON
WATCHING TV
UNDOUBTEDLY IS.

Now arrange the circled letters to form the
surprise answer, as suggested by the above
cartoon.

Print
answer
here

A "⬡⬡⬡⬡" ⬡⬡⬡⬡⬡⬡⬡

JUMBLE®

Unscramble these four Jumbles, one letter to each square, to form four ordinary words.

TILUQ

EGGOR

HANKES

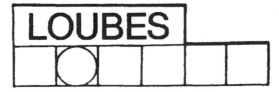

LOUBES

WHY THEY ALWAYS ACCUSED HIM OF BEING NEGATIVE.

Now arrange the circled letters to form the surprise answer, as suggested by the above cartoon.

Print answer here   HE WAS A " ⬚⬚ - ⬚⬚ - ⬚⬚⬚ "

JUMBLE®

Unscramble these four Jumbles, one letter to each square, to form four ordinary words.

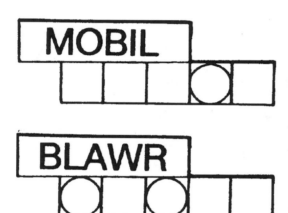

MOBIL

BLAWR

EURUFT

PHONTY

WHEN IT COMES TO A DISHWASHER, MOST EVERY HUSBAND WOULD RATHER DO THIS.

Now arrange the circled letters to form the surprise answer, as suggested by the above cartoon.

Print answer here

JUMBLE®

Unscramble these four Jumbles, one letter to each square, to form four ordinary words.

JABON

OVERP

EVIDID

THINEZ

WHAT THE
HULA DANCER
DID TO THE GUYS
IN THE AUDIENCE.

Now arrange the circled letters to form the surprise answer, as suggested by the above cartoon.

Print answer here " ◯◯◯ – ◯◯◯◯◯◯◯◯ " 'EM

JUMBLE®

Unscramble these four Jumbles, one letter to
each square, to form four ordinary words.

GIMED

YUNTT

YORCAN

BLUESH

WHAT HER
STEADY DATE WAS
MUCH OF THE TIME.

Now arrange the circled letters to form the
surprise answer, as suggested by the above
cartoon.

Print answer here

JUMBLE®

Unscramble these four Jumbles, one letter to
each square, to form four ordinary words.

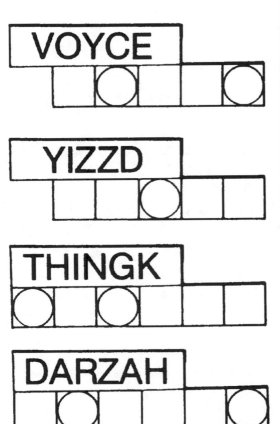

VOYCE

YIZZD

THINGK

DARZAH

I don't believe
a word of it

WHAT ALL THAT
TALK ABOUT
HOROSCOPES WAS.

Now arrange the circled letters to form the
surprise answer, as suggested by the above
cartoon.

Print answer here

JUMBLE®

Unscramble these four Jumbles, one letter to
each square, to form four ordinary words.

VALIT

SELOO

LOCHOS

RATTAR

BARGAIN
INVESTMENTS

WHAT THE DISCOUNT
REAL ESTATE BROKER
OFFERED TO SELL.

Now arrange the circled letters to form the
surprise answer, as suggested by the above
cartoon.

*Print
answer
here* " ⬡⬡⬡⬡ " FOR ⬡⬡⬡⬡⬡⬡

JUMBLE®

Unscramble these four Jumbles, one letter to
each square, to form four ordinary words.

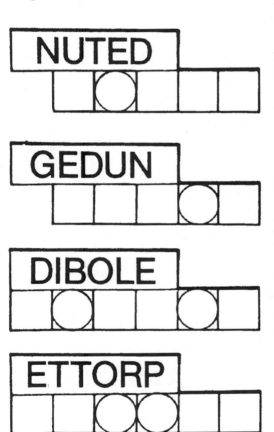

NUTED

GEDUN

DIBOLE

ETTORP

They're all
the same

THAT DOOR-TO-DOOR
SALESMAN GOT
ONLY ONE ORDER—

Now arrange the circled letters to form the
surprise answer, as suggested by the above
cartoon.

Print answer here " ☐◯◯☐ ◯◯◯☐ ! "

15

JUMBLE®

Unscramble these four Jumbles, one letter to
each square, to form four ordinary words.

BOANT

SINOE

NEDDAW

LAHRDY

Any guy who goes
out with her is
asking for it

DRUGS
COSMETICS

WHY THEY CALLED
HER A SUICIDE
BLONDE.

Now arrange the circled letters to form the
surprise answer, as suggested by the above
cartoon.

*Print
answer
here* " ☐☐☐☐ " BY
HER ☐☐☐ ☐☐☐☐

JUMBLE®

Unscramble these four Jumbles, one letter to
each square, to form four ordinary words.

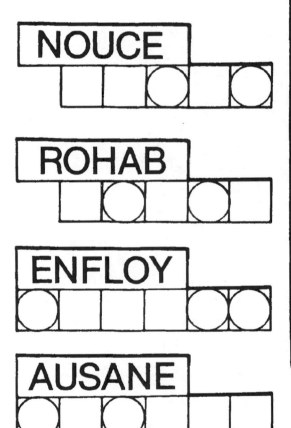

NOUCE

ROHAB

ENFLOY

AUSANE

HE LAUGHED UP
HIS SLEEVE
BECAUSE THAT'S
WHERE THIS WAS.

Now arrange the circled letters to form the
surprise answer, as suggested by the above
cartoon.

Print answer here HIS

JUMBLE®

Unscramble these four Jumbles, one letter to
each square, to form four ordinary words.

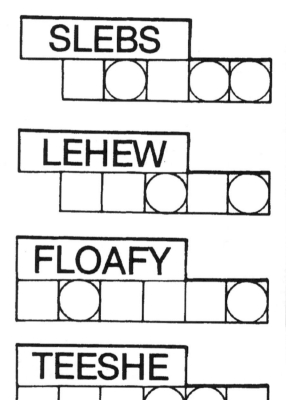

SLEBS

LEHEW

FLOAFY

TEESHE

WHY BUSINESS IS
ALWAYS GOOD FOR
THE VENDOR OF
PEANUTS.

Now arrange the circled letters to form the
surprise answer, as suggested by the above
cartoon.

Print
answer THEY "◯◯◯◯◯◯" ◯◯◯◯
here

JUMBLE®

Unscramble these four Jumbles, one letter to each square, to form four ordinary words.

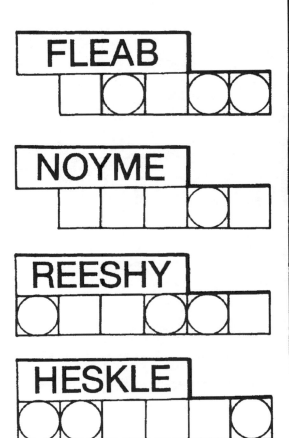

FLEAB

NOYME

REESHY

HESKLE

WHAT A FOOT DOCTOR SOME-TIMES DOES.

Now arrange the circled letters to form the surprise answer, as suggested by the above cartoon.

Print answer here " "

JUMBLE®

Unscramble these four Jumbles, one letter to
each square, to form four ordinary words.

CEMIN

LEXEP

MAINEA

DEWIST

I'm going
out shopping

A COUNTERFEITER
IS THE ONLY MAN
IN THE WORLD
WHO MAKES MORE
MONEY THAN THIS.

5-27

Now arrange the circled letters to form the
surprise answer, as suggested by the above
cartoon.

Print answer here ANYONE ⬡⬡⬡ ⬡⬡⬡⬡⬡

JUMBLE®

Unscramble these four Jumbles, one letter to
each square, to form four ordinary words.

IMECH

DANGL

FLANEL

REVABE

JEALOUSY SETS
IN WITH THE
ARRIVAL OF THIS.

Now arrange the circled letters to form the
surprise answer, as suggested by the above
cartoon.

Print answer here

JUMBLE®

Unscramble these four Jumbles, one letter to each square, to form four ordinary words.

MENOG

KASHY

SACULE

CEITED

As I always said, he's got a great future

THE "GO-GETTER" KNOWS THAT THE RULES FOR GETTING AHEAD WON'T WORK UNLESS THIS HAPPENS.

Now arrange the circled letters to form the surprise answer, as suggested by the above cartoon.

Print answer here

JUMBLE®

Unscramble these four Jumbles, one letter to each square, to form four ordinary words.

WYSON

RYMEE

NATIED

TOGIER

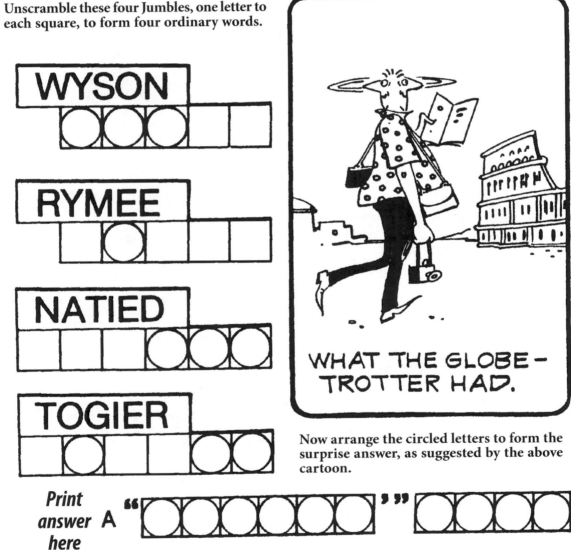

WHAT THE GLOBE-TROTTER HAD.

Now arrange the circled letters to form the surprise answer, as suggested by the above cartoon.

Print answer here   A " ⬡⬡⬡⬡⬡⬡ " ⬡⬡⬡⬡

JUMBLE®

Unscramble these four Jumbles, one letter to each square, to form four ordinary words.

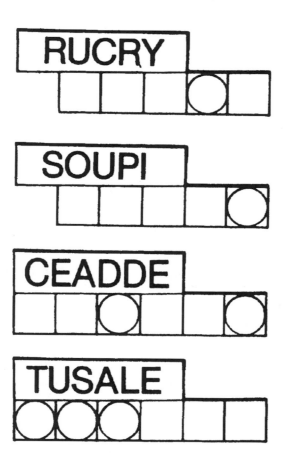

RUCRY

SOUPI

CEADDE

TUSALE

Hello. . . Insurance company?

HOW CARELESS DRIVERS FREQUENTLY END UP.

Now arrange the circled letters to form the surprise answer, as suggested by the above cartoon.

Print answer here " ⃝⃝⃝⃝⃝⃝⃝ "

JUMBLE®

Unscramble these four Jumbles, one letter to each square, to form four ordinary words.

CHABT

TALEE

EUGLED

FEWURC

He's sure gone far

WHAT THAT "GO-GETTER" FINALLY MANAGED TO DO.

Now arrange the circled letters to form the surprise answer, as suggested by the above cartoon.

Print answer here " ⃝⃝⃝ ⃝⃝⃝ "

JUMBLE®

Unscramble these four Jumbles, one letter to each square, to form four ordinary words.

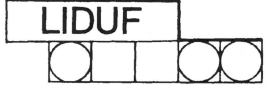

LIDUF

ESHOU

POOPSE

SLAQUL

WHAT THE FEMALE DINOSAUR SAID TO HER GROUCHY MATE.

Now arrange the circled letters to form the surprise answer, as suggested by the above cartoon.

Print answer here YOU ⬤⬤⬤ ⬤⬤⬤⬤⬤⬤

Jumpin' JUMBLE®

Daily Puzzles

JUMBLE®

Unscramble these four Jumbles, one letter to each square, to form four ordinary words.

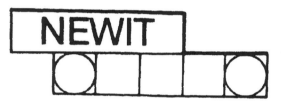

NEWIT

VINEA

LEETEY

ISSUME

THE CROWD DID THIS WHEN THE WINNING TEAM PASSED BY.

Now arrange the circled letters to form the surprise answer, as suggested by the above cartoon.

Print answer here

 OFF "  "

JUMBLE®

Unscramble these four Jumbles, one letter to each square, to form four ordinary words.

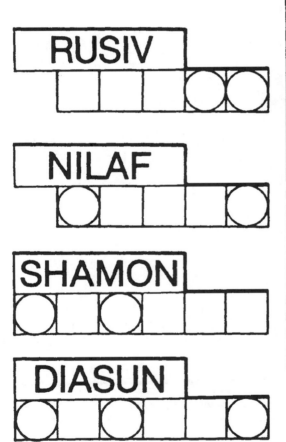

RUSIV

NILAF

SHAMON

DIASUN

But where will the money come from?

I think I've got an idea

WHAT THE CITY REQUIRED IN ORDER TO CLEAN UP THE AFTERMATH OF A BIG SNOWSTORM.

Now arrange the circled letters to form the surprise answer, as suggested by the above cartoon.

Print answer here A " ◯◯◯◯◯ " ◯◯◯◯

JUMBLE®

Unscramble these four Jumbles, one letter to each square, to form four ordinary words.

MIDUH

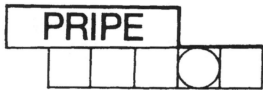

PRIPE

YETTIN

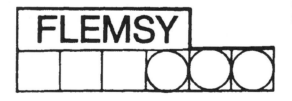

FLEMSY

Villa Ristorante

FAT IS THE PENALTY FOR EXCEEDING THIS.

Now arrange the circled letters to form the surprise answer, as suggested by the above cartoon.

Print answer here THE

JUMBLE®

Unscramble these four Jumbles, one letter to
each square, to form four ordinary words.

EKRIP

TAULD

EUMMUS

REVUPY

He really knows
how to perform
tricks

WHAT THEY
CALLED THAT
GREAT MAGICIAN.

Now arrange the circled letters to form the
surprise answer, as suggested by the above
cartoon.

Print
answer A
here

JUMBLE®

Unscramble these four Jumbles, one letter to each square, to form four ordinary words.

CHARP

SMACH

ZARABA

LIMUHE

ANOTHER NAME FOR RABBIT FUR.

Now arrange the circled letters to form the surprise answer, as suggested by the above cartoon.

Print answer here ⭕⭕⭕⭕ ⭕⭕⭕⭕

JUMBLE

Unscramble these four Jumbles, one letter to
each square, to form four ordinary words.

ACEEP

CHOAR

NOWWIN

LIRMAN

There's work to be done
out there, dear

BONDS STOCKS

THEY USED TO
CONSIDER HIM A
"RAKE," BUT NOW
HE'S SIMPLY
TURNED INTO THIS,

Now arrange the circled letters to form the
surprise answer, as suggested by the above
cartoon.

Print answer here A

33

JUMBLE®

Unscramble these four Jumbles, one letter to each square, to form four ordinary words.

CHATY

YURMK

KLUNIE

GOFERR

HE BUILT A GOOD FIRE, AND SHE SAID THIS.

Now arrange the circled letters to form the surprise answer, as suggested by the above cartoon.

Print answer here "  – ! "

JUMBLE®

Unscramble these four Jumbles, one letter to
each square, to form four ordinary words.

VENOW

HAKSY

TOOCLE

HOPOUK

Wasn't
fast enough
with those
punches

THE BOXING RING
IS NO PLACE
FOR THIS.

Now arrange the circled letters to form the
surprise answer, as suggested by the above
cartoon.

Print answer here A ⬡⬡⬡⬡⬡ " ⬡⬡⬡⬡ "

JUMBLE

Unscramble these four Jumbles, one letter to each square, to form four ordinary words.

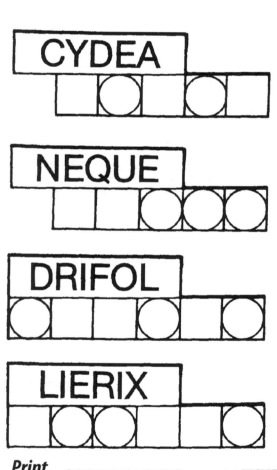

CYDEA

NEQUE

DRIFOL

LIERIX

Uh, oh...
I'd better
scram

**WHAT THE STAG
DID WHEN THE
HUNTERS ARRIVED.**

Now arrange the circled letters to form the surprise answer, as suggested by the above cartoon.

Print answer here

 FOR "  "

JUMBLE®

Unscramble these four Jumbles, one letter to
each square, to form four ordinary words.

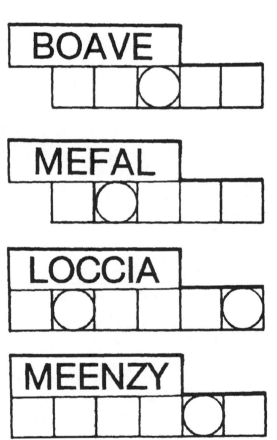

BOAVE

MEFAL

LOCCIA

MEENZY

WHAT THE BIG
DAIRY FARMER
HAD LOTS OF.

Now arrange the circled letters to form the
surprise answer, as suggested by the above
cartoon.

Print answer here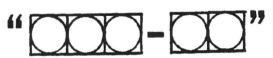

JUMBLE®

Unscramble these four Jumbles, one letter to
each square, to form four ordinary words.

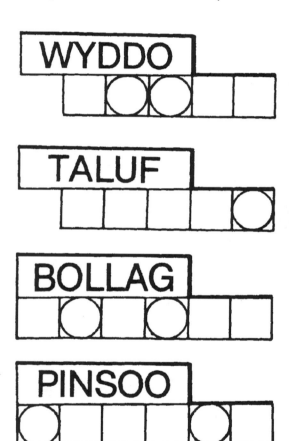

WYDDO

TALUF

BOLLAG

PINSOO

WHAT SHE PROCEEDED
TO DO AFTER HER
BOYFRIEND CANCELED
THEIR DATE.

Now arrange the circled letters to form the
surprise answer, as suggested by the above
cartoon.

Print answer here

JUMBLE®

Unscramble these four Jumbles, one letter to each square, to form four ordinary words.

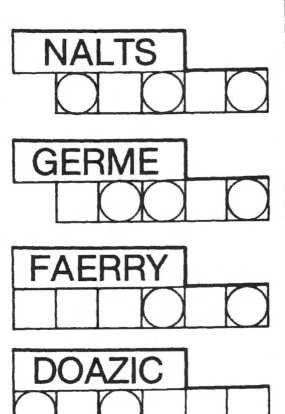

NALTS

GERME

FAERRY

DOAZIC

Those songs were popular around the time we got married

Everything was much better then

ANOTHER NAME FOR NOSTALGIA.

Now arrange the circled letters to form the surprise answer, as suggested by the above cartoon.

Print answer here " ◯◯◯◯◯◯◯◯◯◯ "

JUMBLE®

Unscramble these four Jumbles, one letter to each square, to form four ordinary words.

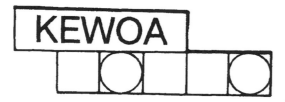

KEWOA

LIPTO

TERVOX

ENDOTE

HE COULDN'T SWIM A STROKE, BUT HE KNEW THIS.

Now arrange the circled letters to form the surprise answer, as suggested by the above cartoon.

Print answer here EVERY  " " IN

JUMBLE®

Unscramble these four Jumbles, one letter to
each square, to form four ordinary words.

CIEPE

YANDS

LYNKIG

PANMEC

Did he
learn
anything
else?

THEIR KID'S COLLEGE
EDUCATION SEEMED
TO BE JUST THIS.

Now arrange the circled letters to form the
surprise answer, as suggested by the above
cartoon.

Print answer here

JUMBLE®

Unscramble these four Jumbles, one letter to
each square, to form four ordinary words.

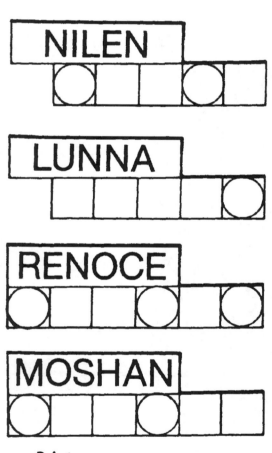

NILEN

LUNNA

RENOCE

MOSHAN

WHAT THAT
BLACKGUARD WAS.

Now arrange the circled letters to form the
surprise answer, as suggested by the above
cartoon.

Print answer here A ◯◯◯◯ WITHOUT " ◯◯◯◯ "
A

JUMBLE®

Unscramble these four Jumbles, one letter to
each square, to form four ordinary words.

INWET
◯◯☐☐

KICCH
☐◯◯☐

FRIMIN
☐☐☐☐◯◯

HELBED
☐◯◯☐◯

At least she's doing
something about it

—

SHE WENT TO
SOME LENGTH
TO CHANGE THIS.

Now arrange the circled letters to form the
surprise answer, as suggested by the above
cartoon.

Print answer here ◯◯◯ ◯◯◯◯◯

JUMBLE®

Unscramble these four Jumbles, one letter to each square, to form four ordinary words.

RAFIE

OAPIN

AGGIZZ

EMFONT

He doesn't know what he's talking about

LIKE A SHIP, SOME SPEAKERS TOOT LOUDEST WHEN THEY'RE THIS.

Now arrange the circled letters to form the surprise answer, as suggested by the above cartoon.

Print answer here

JUMBLE®

Unscramble these four Jumbles, one letter to each square, to form four ordinary words.

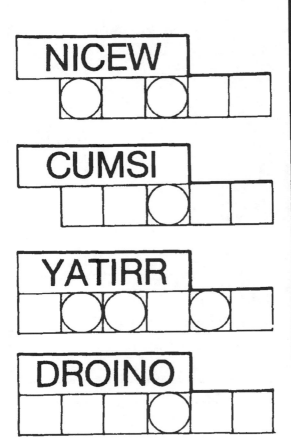

NICEW

CUMSI

YATIRR

DROINO

A POLITICIAN IS A MAN WHO'S SWORN INTO OFFICE AND THEN THIS AFTERWARD.

Now arrange the circled letters to form the surprise answer, as suggested by the above cartoon.

Print answer here

JUMBLE®

Unscramble these four Jumbles, one letter to
each square, to form four ordinary words.

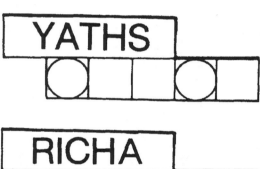

YATHS

RICHA

LUMUTT

DOSTIL

YOU CAN LOSE
WEIGHT BEST BY NOT
TALKING ABOUT IT,
BUT BY KEEPING
THIS.

Now arrange the circled letters to form the
surprise answer, as suggested by the above
cartoon.

Print answer here YOUR

JUMBLE®

Unscramble these four Jumbles, one letter to
each square, to form four ordinary words.

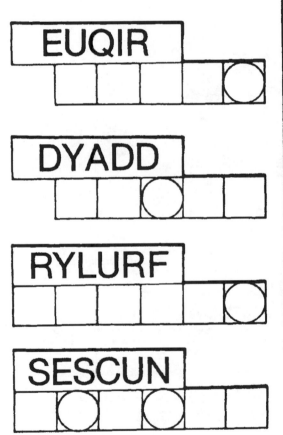

EUQIR

DYADD

RYLURF

SESCUN

A YOUNG MAN WHO
SPENDS TOO MUCH
TIME SOWING HIS
WILD OATS MIGHT
BEGIN TO LOOK THIS.

Now arrange the circled letters to form the
surprise answer, as suggested by the above
cartoon.

Print answer here " ⬡⬡⬡⬡⬡ "

JUMBLE®

Unscramble these four Jumbles, one letter to each square, to form four ordinary words.

LOOFI

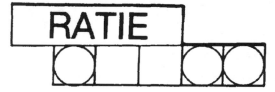

RATIE

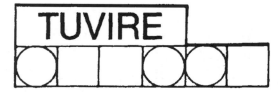

TUVIRE

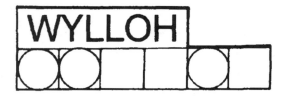

WYLLOH

Africa   Paris   South America

TOURS

We're going to the lake, as usual

A FAMILY THAT LIVES WITHIN ITS INCOME USUALLY HAS TO LEARN TO DO THIS.

Now arrange the circled letters to form the surprise answer, as suggested by the above cartoon.

Print answer here

JUMBLE®

Unscramble these four Jumbles, one letter to
each square, to form four ordinary words.

SELLI

AGDEA

BRAJEB

DOBOLY

Lots of men
of vision here

And
women,
too

WHAT THE
OPHTHALMOLOGISTS
CALLED THEIR
ANNUAL SHINDIG.

Now arrange the circled letters to form the
surprise answer, as suggested by the above
cartoon.

Print answer here THE " ☐☐☐ ☐☐☐☐ "

JUMBLE®

Unscramble these four Jumbles, one letter to each square, to form four ordinary words.

KELLN

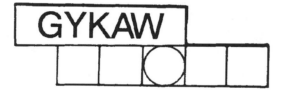
GYKAW

MORLAN

BEATED

OK, dear—we'll go fishing on our honeymoon

THAT ENGAGED COUPLE WAS ON THE VERGE OF BREAKING UP BEFORE SHE FINALLY MANAGED TO DO THIS.

Now arrange the circled letters to form the surprise answer, as suggested by the above cartoon.

Print answer here ⬡⬡⬡⬡⬡ HIM ⬡⬡⬡⬡

JUMBLE®

Unscramble these four Jumbles, one letter to each square, to form four ordinary words.

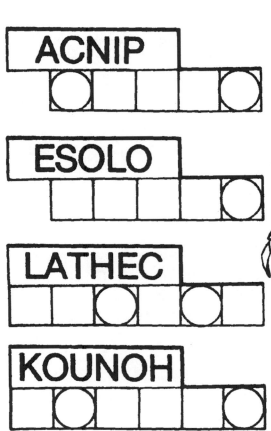

ACNIP

ESOLO

LATHEC

KOUNOH

**WHAT CAP IS
NEVER REMOVED?**

Now arrange the circled letters to form the surprise answer, as suggested by the above cartoon.

Print answer here THE ⭕⭕⭕⭕⭕⭕⭕

JUMBLE®

Unscramble these four Jumbles, one letter to each square, to form four ordinary words.

TYREN

YIRNB

RUGEDD

DELNAH

WHAT THE FORMERLY "HEAVY" CLIENT AT THE REDUCING SALON SAID AFTER SHE LOST ALL THAT WEIGHT.

Now arrange the circled letters to form the surprise answer, as suggested by the above cartoon.

Print answer here " ☐☐ – ☐☐☐☐☐ – ☐☐ "

JUMBLE®

Unscramble these four Jumbles, one letter to each square, to form four ordinary words.

NOOZE

HECKE

DUNTIC

WIMDLE

WHAT THE PILLOW TYCOON GOT WHEN BUSINESS WAS BAD.

Now arrange the circled letters to form the surprise answer, as suggested by the above cartoon.

Print answer here " ⬡⬡⬡⬡ " IN THE ⬡⬡⬡⬡⬡

JUMBLE®

Unscramble these four Jumbles, one letter to
each square, to form four ordinary words.

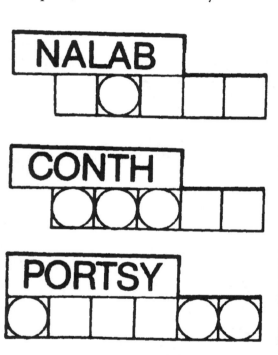

NALAB

CONTH

PORTSY

GRACIT

OFFICE SUPPLIES

WHEN PRICES ON
EVERYTHING ELSE
WENT UP AT THAT
STORE, ENVELOPES
REMAINED THIS.

Now arrange the circled letters to form the
surprise answer, as suggested by the above
cartoon.

Print answer here " ◯◯◯◯◯◯◯◯◯◯◯ "

JUMBLE®

Unscramble these four Jumbles, one letter to each square, to form four ordinary words.

CYZAR

YANDD

WOTOWK

VAHLED

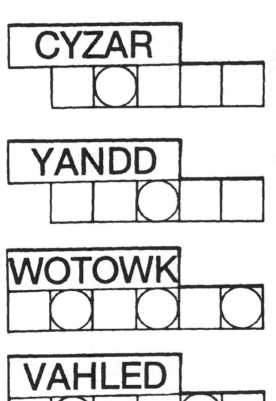

Drink up, everybody—
it's all on me!

HE SPENT HIS
MONEY LIKE WATER
BUT NOT THIS.

Now arrange the circled letters to form the surprise answer, as suggested by the above cartoon.

Print answer here

JUMBLE®

Unscramble these four Jumbles, one letter to each square, to form four ordinary words.

HOOTT

TABLO

MEUGLE

CROSCH

WHERE GRAVE
ROBBERS LEARN
THEIR PROFESSION.

Now arrange the circled letters to form the surprise answer, as suggested by the above cartoon.

Print answer here IN

JUMBLE

Unscramble these four Jumbles, one letter to
each square, to form four ordinary words.

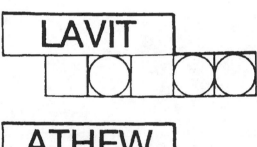

LAVIT

ATHEW

LOSFIS

DRENER

WHAT AN AIRLINE
MIGHT DO IN ORDER
TO DRUM UP
BUSINESS.

Now arrange the circled letters to form the
surprise answer, as suggested by the above
cartoon.

Print
answer
here
 OUT " "

JUMBLE®

Unscramble these four Jumbles, one letter to each square, to form four ordinary words.

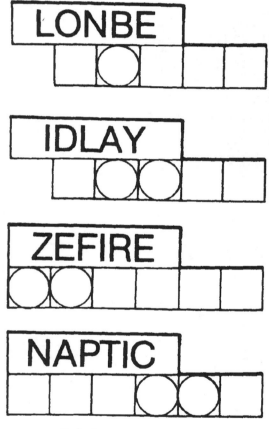

LONBE

IDLAY

ZEFIRE

NAPTIC

WHAT HAPPENS WHEN TWO EGOTISTS HAVE A FALLING OUT.

Now arrange the circled letters to form the surprise answer, as suggested by the above cartoon.

Print answer here

IT'S ⬡⬡ " ⬡ " ⬡⬡⬡ AN " ⬡ "

JUMBLE®

Unscramble these four Jumbles, one letter to
each square, to form four ordinary words.

SUMEO

LAVIA

YOGAVE

SAUNAE

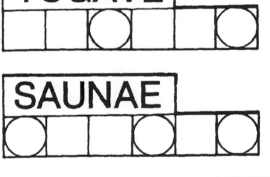

My husband will be
so proud of me

BARGAIN
SALE

SHE'S DETERMINED
TO DO THIS, NO
MATTER HOW MUCH
IT COSTS.

Now arrange the circled letters to form the
surprise answer, as suggested by the above
cartoon.

Print answer here

JUMBLE®

Unscramble these four Jumbles, one letter to each square, to form four ordinary words.

YURLS

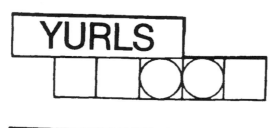

NEESU

CLAGEY

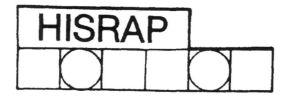

HISRAP

Let's destroy 'em!

WHAT DID THEY CALL THE TEAM MADE UP OF FRANKENSTEIN MONSTERS?

Now arrange the circled letters to form the surprise answer, as suggested by the above cartoon.

Print answer here THE "  "

JUMBLE®

Unscramble these four Jumbles, one letter to
each square, to form four ordinary words.

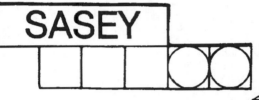

SASEY

RUZEA

HYCTOU

GERELD

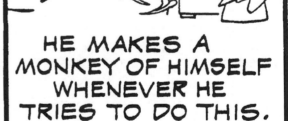

Wait'll you hear this!

HE MAKES A
MONKEY OF HIMSELF
WHENEVER HE
TRIES TO DO THIS.

Now arrange the circled letters to form the
surprise answer, as suggested by the above
cartoon.

Print answer here ⬡⬡⬡⬡⬡ A " ⬡⬡⬡⬡ "

JUMBLE

Unscramble these four Jumbles, one letter to each square, to form four ordinary words.

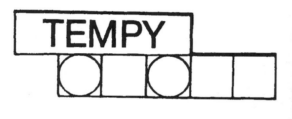

TEMPY

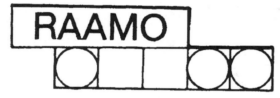

RAAMO

CLIPEN

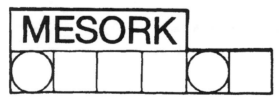

MESORK

WHY THE WORMS DIDN'T ENTER NOAH'S ARK IN "PAIRS."

Now arrange the circled letters to form the surprise answer, as suggested by the above cartoon.

Print answer here THEY ⬡⬡⬡⬡ IN ⬡⬡⬡⬡⬡⬡

JUMBLE®

Unscramble these four Jumbles, one letter to each square, to form four ordinary words.

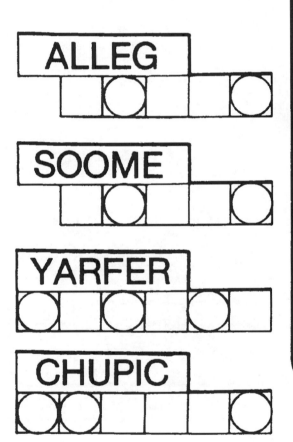

ALLEG

SOOME

YARFER

CHUPIC

PRAISE THIS AND YOU'RE SURE TO TURN A WOMAN'S HEAD.

Now arrange the circled letters to form the surprise answer, as suggested by the above cartoon.

Print answer here

JUMBLE®

Unscramble these four Jumbles, one letter to each square, to form four ordinary words.

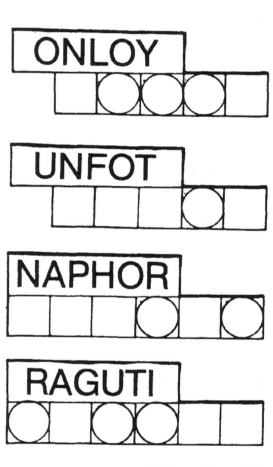

ONLOY

UNFOT

NAPHOR

RAGUTI

Ho hum

WHY THEY FOUND THE NUDIST CAMP SO BORING.

Now arrange the circled letters to form the surprise answer, as suggested by the above cartoon.

Print answer here  WENT

JUMBLE®

Unscramble these four Jumbles, one letter to each square, to form four ordinary words.

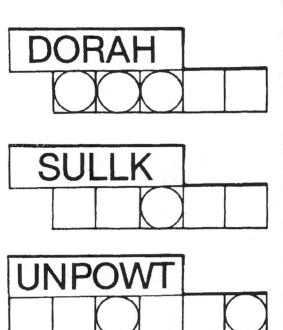

DORAH

SULLK

UNPOWT

RIDOLF

HOW THE MANICURIST REJECTED HIS PROPOSAL OF MARRIAGE.

Now arrange the circled letters to form the surprise answer, as suggested by the above cartoon.

Print answer here

JUMBLE®

Unscramble these four Jumbles, one letter to each square, to form four ordinary words.

LINAF

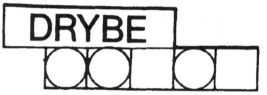

DRYBE

UNNACE

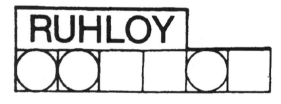

RUHLOY

ANOTHER NAME FOR A DIALOGUE.

Now arrange the circled letters to form the surprise answer, as suggested by the above cartoon.

Print answer here   A  "  "

JUMBLE®

Unscramble these four Jumbles, one letter to
each square, to form four ordinary words.

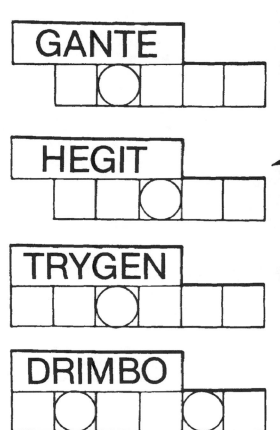

GANTE

HEGIT

TRYGEN

DRIMBO

SHE WAS ALWAYS
SURE TO KEEP
A SECRET...

Now arrange the circled letters to form the
surprise answer, as suggested by the above
cartoon.

Print answer here

JUMBLE®

Unscramble these four Jumbles, one letter to each square, to form four ordinary words.

DAHEA

BICAN

SCOFIA

PIMNED

APPARENTLY IT'S A SIGN OF GOOD MANNERS TO PUT UP WITH THIS.

Now arrange the circled letters to form the surprise answer, as suggested by the above cartoon.

Print answer here

JUMBLE®

Unscramble these four Jumbles, one letter to
each square, to form four ordinary words.

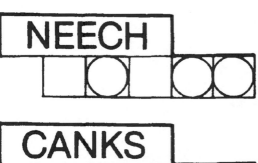

NEECH

CANKS

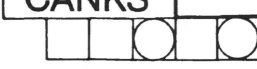

KRABEM

WORDAC

WHEN DID YOU FIRST
NOTICE THAT WEAK BACK?

Now arrange the circled letters to form the
surprise answer, as suggested by the above
cartoon.

Print answer here " ⬡⬡⬡⬡⬡ ⬡⬡⬡⬡ "

JUMBLE®

Unscramble these four Jumbles, one letter to each square, to form four ordinary words.

SUROE

MEFAD

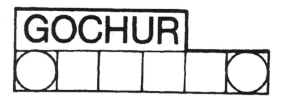

GOCHUR

KOYDEN

You're fired!

Who cares?

THE BAKER LEFT HIS JOB BECAUSE HE DIDN'T THIS.

Now arrange the circled letters to form the surprise answer, as suggested by the above cartoon.

Print answer here

 " ⟨⟩⟨⟩⟨⟩⟨⟩⟨⟩ " THE

JUMBLE®

Unscramble these four Jumbles, one letter to each square, to form four ordinary words.

YIRDT

AGGYB

DEDUIG

ERWANS

WHAT DO YOU GET WHEN A FAT MAN MARRIES A FAT LADY?

Now arrange the circled letters to form the surprise answer, as suggested by the above cartoon.

Print answer here A ⬭⬭⬭ ⬭⬭⬭⬭⬭⬭⬭

JUMBLE®

Unscramble these four Jumbles, one letter to each square, to form four ordinary words.

HECEL

RUJOR

VITEOM

FLERBY

WHAT YOU MIGHT EXPECT HIM TO DO WHEN SHE SPENDS ALL THAT MONEY ON SOME SILLY ART OBJECT.

Now arrange the circled letters to form the surprise answer, as suggested by the above cartoon.

Print answer here

JUMBLE®

Unscramble these four Jumbles, one letter to
each square, to form four ordinary words.

SIPOE

TIHHC

MIESED

YUFEEL

WHAT'S A
MERMAID?

Now arrange the circled letters to form the
surprise answer, as suggested by the above
cartoon.

Print
answer A " ⃝⃝⃝⃝ - ⃝⃝⃝ ⃝⃝⃝⃝ "
here

JUMBLE®

Unscramble these four Jumbles, one letter to each square, to form four ordinary words.

THISO

RAPAT

SAMTIG

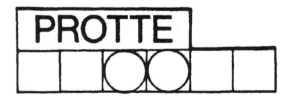
PROTTE

WHAT MANY A NIGHT SPOT IS.

Now arrange the circled letters to form the surprise answer, as suggested by the above cartoon.

Print answer here A " ⬡⬡⬡⬡⬡ " ⬡⬡⬡⬡

JUMBLE®

Unscramble these four Jumbles, one letter to each square, to form four ordinary words.

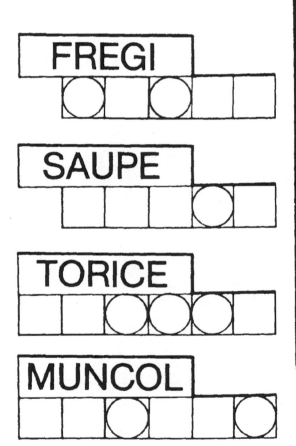

FREGI

SAUPE

TORICE

MUNCOL

No ticket, no coat

YOU CAN'T GET RID OF A BAD TEMPER BY DOING THIS.

Now arrange the circled letters to form the surprise answer, as suggested by the above cartoon.

Print answer here

JUMBLE®

Unscramble these four Jumbles, one letter to each square, to form four ordinary words.

USHOE

WARLC

TOCCUL

HINCUR

ANOTHER NAME FOR THE TIME YOU SPEND GOING HOME FROM WORK.

Now arrange the circled letters to form the surprise answer, as suggested by the above cartoon.

Print answer here THE " ⎡○○○○○⎤ " ⎡○○○○⎤

JUMBLE®

Unscramble these four Jumbles, one letter to
each square, to form four ordinary words.

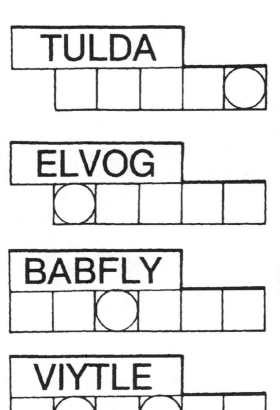

TULDA

ELVOG

BABFLY

VIYTLE

I'd like to read the
prospectus first. I'll
get back to you

ADD THIS ON FOR
YOUR PROTECTION,
IF YOU'RE ABOUT
TO INVEST.

Now arrange the circled letters to form the
surprise answer, as suggested by the above
cartoon.

Print answer here " – ☐☐☐☐☐ "

JUMBLE®

Unscramble these four Jumbles, one letter to each square, to form four ordinary words.

SOSBA

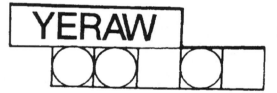
YERAW

LAUTRI

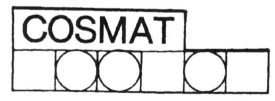
COSMAT

I can guess what he's been up to

HIS CLOTHES TELL YOU A LOT ABOUT THIS.

Now arrange the circled letters to form the surprise answer, as suggested by the above cartoon.

Print answer here

HIS "⬡⬡⬡⬡" – ⬡⬡⬡⬡⬡⬡⬡

JUMBLE®

Unscramble these four Jumbles, one letter to
each square, to form four ordinary words.

STYRT

CAULD

LIRBED

GARNAH

HE'S OLD ENOUGH
TO KNOW BETTER
BUT TOO OLD
TO DO THIS.

Now arrange the circled letters to form the
surprise answer, as suggested by the above
cartoon.

Print answer here

JUMBLE®

Unscramble these four Jumbles, one letter to
each square, to form four ordinary words.

TELLU

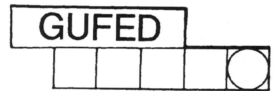

GUFED

SIPVLE

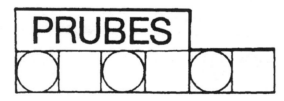

PRUBES

WHAT A GOOD
INSECTICIDE
MIGHT BE.

Now arrange the circled letters to form the
surprise answer, as suggested by the above
cartoon.

Print
answer A " ⃝⃝⃝⃝⃝ " ⃝⃝⃝⃝⃝⃝⃝
here

JUMBLE®

Unscramble these four Jumbles, one letter to each square, to form four ordinary words.

SONDY

ADECK

KLEETT

WHONAY

EVERY DOG HAS ITS "DAY" EXCEPT ONE WITH A SORE TAIL, WHICH HAS THIS.

Now arrange the circled letters to form the surprise answer, as suggested by the above cartoon.

Print answer here ITS " ⬡⬡⬡⬡ ⬡⬡⬡ "

JUMBLE®

Unscramble these four Jumbles, one letter to each square, to form four ordinary words.

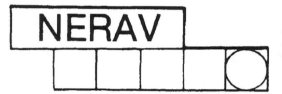

NERAV

BOUMG

EVITLY

CLUGED

Good news!

HOW THEY KNEW THAT THE MAN-EATING SHARK HAD BEEN SHOT DEAD.

Now arrange the circled letters to form the surprise answer, as suggested by the above cartoon.

Print answer here   THERE WAS A "  "

JUMBLE®

Unscramble these four Jumbles, one letter to each square, to form four ordinary words.

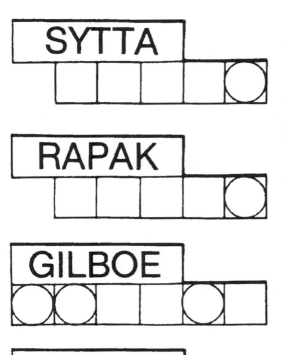

SYTTA

RAPAK

GILBOE

BLOUED

Best suit sale we ever had

WHY THE SHOPKEEPER SAID FAREWELL TO THAT BARGAIN MERCHANDISE.

Now arrange the circled letters to form the surprise answer, as suggested by the above cartoon.

Print answer here IT WAS " ☐☐☐☐☐ ☐☐☐ "

JUMBLE®

Unscramble these four Jumbles, one letter to
each square, to form four ordinary words.

NULCE

POZAT

HANPOR

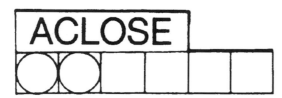

ACLOSE

THAT DUMBBELL WAS
PLANNING TO PUT HIS
FEET INTO THE OVEN
IN ORDER TO DO THIS.

Now arrange the circled letters to form the
surprise answer, as suggested by the above
cartoon.

 *Print answer here* ☐◯◯◯ HIS ◯☐◯◯◯◯◯

JUMBLE®

Unscramble these four Jumbles, one letter to each square, to form four ordinary words.

MYDUP

CHEEN

BRUBRE

GREFOT

FINE FOODS

THE RESTAURANT ACROSS FROM THE THEATER WAS ALWAYS PACKED BECAUSE THE PLAY WAS STRICTLY THIS.

Now arrange the circled letters to form the surprise answer, as suggested by the above cartoon.

Print answer here " ◯◯◯◯ ◯◯◯◯◯◯ "

85

JUMBLE

Unscramble these four Jumbles, one letter to
each square, to form four ordinary words.

OMBOL

FONTE

DRUSAB

MUGLEE

He never acts
that way
at home

**WHAT KIND OF
PERSONALITY DID
THAT CHAMPION
FENCER HAVE?**

Now arrange the circled letters to form the
surprise answer, as suggested by the above
cartoon.

Print answer here A " ☐☐☐☐☐ " ☐☐☐

JUMBLE®

Unscramble these four Jumbles, one letter to each square, to form four ordinary words.

LAINF

SOMEO

LETHAH

NYFLOD

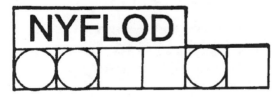

Take your gifts and get out!

Ordinarily, he's very smart

WHAT A MAN IN LOVE SOMETIMES SHOWS GREAT INGENUITY IN MAKING.

Now arrange the circled letters to form the surprise answer, as suggested by the above cartoon.

Print answer here

A ◯◯◯◯◯ OF ◯◯◯◯◯◯◯◯

JUMBLE®

Unscramble these four Jumbles, one letter to each square, to form four ordinary words.

KORBO

YADDD

RADIOT

SELAMY

They love to hiss him —

THAT BELOVED MOVIE VILLAIN WAS SO GOOD AT BEING THIS.

Now arrange the circled letters to form the surprise answer, as suggested by the above cartoon.

Print answer here

JUMBLE®

Unscramble these four Jumbles, one letter to each square, to form four ordinary words.

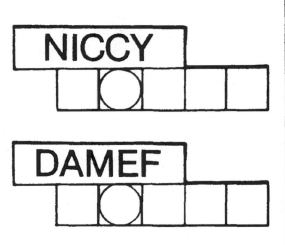

NICCY

DAMEF

LARREB

PARTUB

HOW THE BACKSEAT DRIVER'S HUSBAND DROVE.

Now arrange the circled letters to form the surprise answer, as suggested by the above cartoon.

Print answer here

JUMBLE®

Unscramble these four Jumbles, one letter to each square, to form four ordinary words.

YASSA

GULEN

DIRNEH

SYPEDE

RICH FOOD,
LIKE DESTINY,
CAN DO THIS.

Now arrange the circled letters to form the surprise answer, as suggested by the above cartoon.

Print answer here ⬚⬚⬚⬚⬚ OUR ⬚⬚⬚⬚

JUMBLE®

Unscramble these four Jumbles, one letter to
each square, to form four ordinary words.

GILEA

BAINC

FLASTE

COORTH

THEY NAMED THEIR
TEAM THE SPIDERS
BECAUSE ALL OF
THEM KNEW HOW
TO DO THIS.

Now arrange the circled letters to form the
surprise answer, as suggested by the above
cartoon.

Print answer here

JUMBLE®

Unscramble these four Jumbles, one letter to
each square, to form four ordinary words.

NAGET

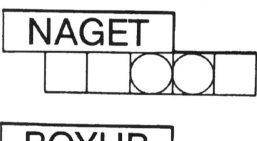

BOYHB

PUMITE

SOWDRY

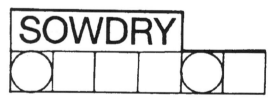

WHAT THAT UNDER-
COVER AGENT WAS
ALSO KNOWN AS.

Now arrange the circled letters to form the
surprise answer, as suggested by the above
cartoon.

Print answer here A

JUMBLE®

Unscramble these four Jumbles, one letter to each square, to form four ordinary words.

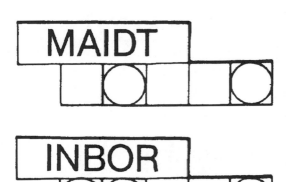

MAIDT

INBOR

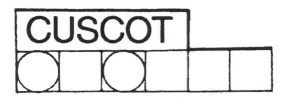

CUSCOT

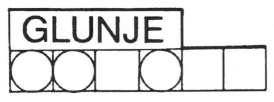

GLUNJE

THIS COFFEE TASTES LIKE MUD!

Now arrange the circled letters to form the surprise answer, as suggested by the above cartoon.

Print answer here

"IT WAS " "

JUMBLE®

Unscramble these four Jumbles, one letter to each square, to form four ordinary words.

NOAGY

MUGAT

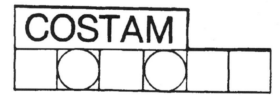

COSTAM

SLOIPH

C'mon—speak up!

THE HYPOCHONDRIAC SAID HE WAS SO SICK HE COULDN'T EVEN DO THIS.

Now arrange the circled letters to form the surprise answer, as suggested by the above cartoon.

Print answer here

JUMBLE®

Unscramble these four Jumbles, one letter to each square, to form four ordinary words.

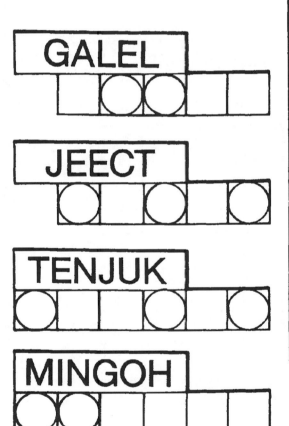

GALEL

JEECT

TENJUK

MINGOH

HE WHO LAUGHS LAST PROBABLY DOESN'T THIS.

Now arrange the circled letters to form the surprise answer, as suggested by the above cartoon.

Print answer here

JUMBLE®

Unscramble these four Jumbles, one letter to each square, to form four ordinary words.

YOVEC
□ □ ◯ □ □

NAGEM
□ ◯ ◯ ◯ □

PINDAK
◯ □ ◯ □ □ □

RUTIVE
□ ◯ □ □ □ ◯

HE MARRIED HER FOR HER LOOKS, BUT NOT THIS.

Now arrange the circled letters to form the surprise answer, as suggested by the above cartoon.

Print answer here THE ◯◯◯◯ SHE OFTEN ◯◯◯◯ HIM

JUMBLE®

Unscramble these four Jumbles, one letter to each square, to form four ordinary words.

NALBA
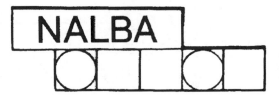

GUVEA

CAFUTE

HANKES

WHAT YOU CAN'T MAKE ON A SLOW HORSE.

Now arrange the circled letters to form the surprise answer, as suggested by the above cartoon.

Print answer here

JUMBLE

Unscramble these four Jumbles, one letter to each square, to form four ordinary words.

HOPUC

TRYAR

SNODEC

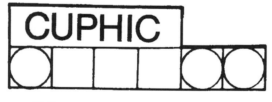
CUPHIC

DRUGS

ANOTHER NAME FOR THAT REDUCING SALON.

Now arrange the circled letters to form the surprise answer, as suggested by the above cartoon.

Print answer here THE "⬡⬡⬡⬡⬡⬡" ⬡⬡⬡⬡

JUMBLE®

Unscramble these four Jumbles, one letter to each square, to form four ordinary words.

KNARC

HYNIS

YELMIT

SWEFET

OFTEN DROPPED BUT SELDOM PICKED UP.

Now arrange the circled letters to form the surprise answer, as suggested by the above cartoon.

Print answer here ◯◯◯◯◯

JUMBLE®

Unscramble these four Jumbles, one letter to each square, to form four ordinary words.

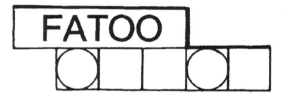

FATOO

AXMMI

TANCAV

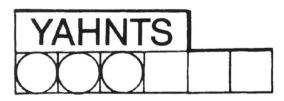

YAHNTS

WHAT THEY CALLED THAT WEALTHY PLAYBOY.

Now arrange the circled letters to form the surprise answer, as suggested by the above cartoon.

Print answer here " ◯◯◯◯ – ◯◯◯◯◯ "

JUMBLE®

Unscramble these four Jumbles, one letter to
each square, to form four ordinary words.

GOGSY

CRANF

MECION

COMIAT

IT'S HARD TO
RAISE A CHILD,
ESPECIALLY WHEN
IT'S THIS.

Now arrange the circled letters to form the
surprise answer, as suggested by the above
cartoon.

Print answer here

JUMBLE®

Unscramble these four Jumbles, one letter to each square, to form four ordinary words.

BLAYK

DIXEO

BIFCAR

ENPLYT

A BUSINESSMAN IS JUDGED BY THE COMPANY HE KEEPS...

Now arrange the circled letters to form the surprise answer, as suggested by the above cartoon.

Print answer here

JUMBLE®

Unscramble these four Jumbles, one letter to each square, to form four ordinary words.

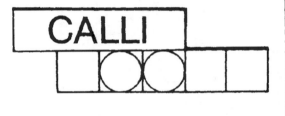

CALLI

WOPER

TAMENG

RUBENK

THAT BORE WON'T STOP TALKING UNTIL YOU START THIS.

Now arrange the circled letters to form the surprise answer, as suggested by the above cartoon.

Print answer here

JUMBLE®

Unscramble these four Jumbles, one letter to
each square, to form four ordinary words.

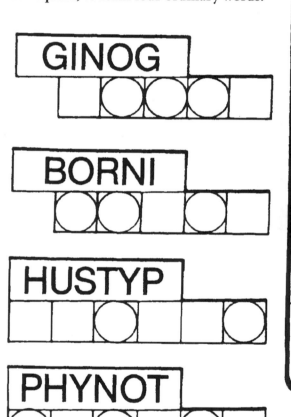

GINOG

BORNI

HUSTYP

PHYNOT

HOW HE USUALLY
ENDED A SENTENCE.

Now arrange the circled letters to form the
surprise answer, as suggested by the above
cartoon.

Print
answer   WITH " ⟨ ⟩ "
here   A

JUMBLE®

Unscramble these four Jumbles, one letter to each square, to form four ordinary words.

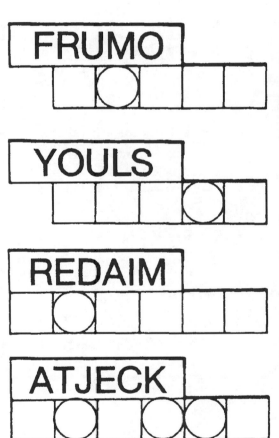

FRUMO

YOULS

REDAIM

ATJECK

Fits you like a glove

WHAT HE GOT WHEN HE BOUGHT THAT "STYLISH" RAINCOAT.

Now arrange the circled letters to form the surprise answer, as suggested by the above cartoon.

Print answer here "  "

105

JUMBLE®

Unscramble these four Jumbles, one letter to
each square, to form four ordinary words.

YAASS

BICCU

RILOAS

FRYTAC

Culture for beginners

WHAT SHE
THOUGHT THAT NEW
FRESHMAN WAS.

Now arrange the circled letters to form the
surprise answer, as suggested by the above
cartoon.

**Print
answer** VERY "◯◯◯◯◯ – ◯◯◯◯◯"
here

JUMBLE

Unscramble these four Jumbles, one letter to
each square, to form four ordinary words.

YUNTT

SNAIB

SLIFSO

CLAGEY

How 'bout dinner tonight?

I'm
tied
up

WHAT HE GOT
FROM THE
SWITCHBOARD
OPERATOR.

Now arrange the circled letters to form the
surprise answer, as suggested by the above
cartoon.

*Print
answer* **THE**
here

JUMBLE®

Unscramble these four Jumbles, one letter to
each square, to form four ordinary words.

SOEBE

MABLY

REMMAH

HYROTE

Any place is better than here

PEOPLE WITH
WANDERLUST SELDOM
FEEL THIS.

Now arrange the circled letters to form the
surprise answer, as suggested by the above
cartoon.

Print answer here AT ⬡⬡⬡⬡ ⬡⬡ ⬡⬡⬡⬡

JUMBLE®

Unscramble these four Jumbles, one letter to each square, to form four ordinary words.

SEGUS

TAREF

DINKAP

BERBOR

Turns my stomach

THE LONGER THAT SERGEANT STAYED IN THE ARMY—

Now arrange the circled letters to form the surprise answer, as suggested by the above cartoon.

Print answer here   THE " ⬡⬡⬡⬡⬡⬡⬡ " HE ⬡⬡⬡

JUMBLE®

Unscramble these four Jumbles, one letter to
each square, to form four ordinary words.

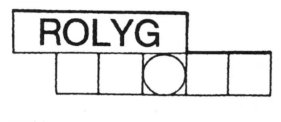

ROLYG

ERNIL

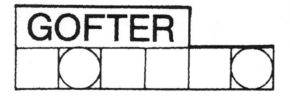

BLABED

GOFTER

WHAT HER ATTEMPTS
AT COOKING
BROUGHT HIM.

Now arrange the circled letters to form the
surprise answer, as suggested by the above
cartoon.

Print answer here

JUMBLE®

Unscramble these four Jumbles, one letter to
each square, to form four ordinary words.

VELDE

CROAG

KEBTUC

NAMALY

WHAT WAS
MICHELANGELO'S
FAVORITE DESSERT?

Now arrange the circled letters to form the
surprise answer, as suggested by the above
cartoon.

Print answer here

111

JUMBLE®

Unscramble these four Jumbles, one letter to
each square, to form four ordinary words.

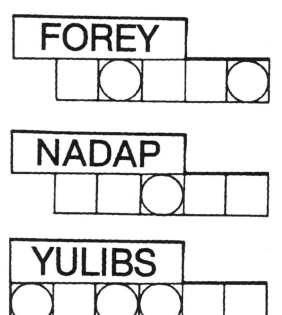

FOREY

NADAP

YULIBS

BELMAG

HOW THE SPONGE
DIVERS FOUND
THEIR WORK.

Now arrange the circled letters to form the
surprise answer, as suggested by the above
cartoon.

Print answer here "〇〇〇〇〇〇〇〇〇"

JUMBLE®

Unscramble these four Jumbles, one letter to each square, to form four ordinary words.

REPIK

TOABB

GAHOME

CRYGLE

Hey—I'm alive!!

WHAT LIGHTNING GAVE THE FRANKENSTEIN MONSTER.

Now arrange the circled letters to form the surprise answer, as suggested by the above cartoon.

Print answer here A ⬡⬡⬡ " ⬡⬡⬡⬡⬡⬡ "

JUMBLE®

Unscramble these four Jumbles, one letter to each square, to form four ordinary words.

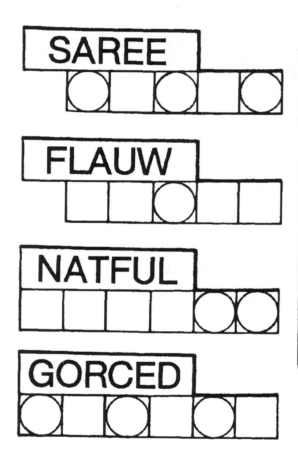

SAREE

FLAUW

NATFUL

GORCED

IT'S NO "FEAT" TO DO THIS.

Now arrange the circled letters to form the surprise answer, as suggested by the above cartoon.

Print answer here ⬡⬡⬡⬡⬡ ON ⬡⬡⬡⬡

JUMBLE®

Unscramble these four Jumbles, one letter to
each square, to form four ordinary words.

STEUG

KLEAF

TARBEN

LICTIE

HE DROVE AS IF HE
OWNED THE ROAD,
WHICH IS WHY HE
ENDED UP NOT
OWNING THIS.

Now arrange the circled letters to form the
surprise answer, as suggested by the above
cartoon.

Print answer here

JUMBLE®

Unscramble these four Jumbles, one letter to each square, to form four ordinary words.

REXET

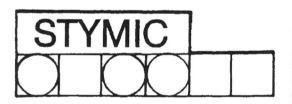

DUGEF

STYMIC

NESTOL

WHAT THE EGOTIST LETS OFF PLENTY OF.

Now arrange the circled letters to form the surprise answer, as suggested by the above cartoon.

Print answer here

□□□□ - □ " □□□□□ "

116

JUMBLE®

Unscramble these four Jumbles, one letter to
each square, to form four ordinary words.

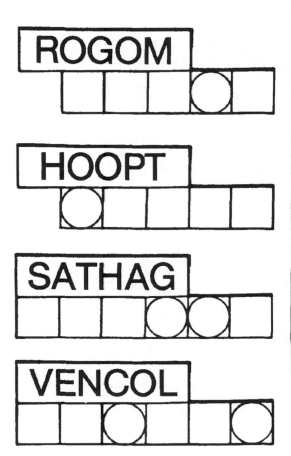

ROGOM

HOOPT

SATHAG

VENCOL

WHAT THE BUBBLE
DANCER SAID WHEN
HE ASKED HER
TO MARRY HIM.

Now arrange the circled letters to form the
surprise answer, as suggested by the above
cartoon.

Print answer here " ◯◯ ◯◯◯◯ "

JUMBLE®

Unscramble these four Jumbles, one letter to
each square, to form four ordinary words.

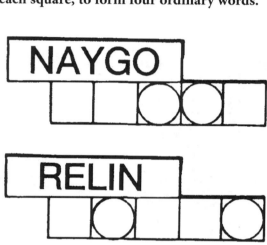

NAYGO

RELIN

YERTAW

GOEMAH

CLOTHES MAKE THE
MAN, ESPECIALLY
WHEN WORN
BY THIS.

Now arrange the circled letters to form the
surprise answer, as suggested by the above
cartoon.

Print
answer THE
here

JUMBLE®

Unscramble these four Jumbles, one letter to each square, to form four ordinary words.

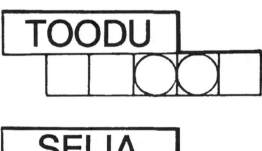
TOODU

SELIA

NOOBBA

PITTEO

Now arrange the circled letters to form the surprise answer, as suggested by the above cartoon.

Print answer here

JUMBLE®

Unscramble these four Jumbles, one letter to each square, to form four ordinary words.

PAUNC

ARCTT

GIRDIF

DOINIE

That's the place where his highness kissed my hand

Next you'll see me dance with the princess

WHAT MANY PEOPLE START OUT ON RIGHT AFTER THEY RETURN HOME FROM A VACATION.

Now arrange the circled letters to form the surprise answer, as suggested by the above cartoon.

Print answer here AN ◯◯◯ ◯◯◯◯

JUMBLE®

Unscramble these four Jumbles, one letter to each square, to form four ordinary words.

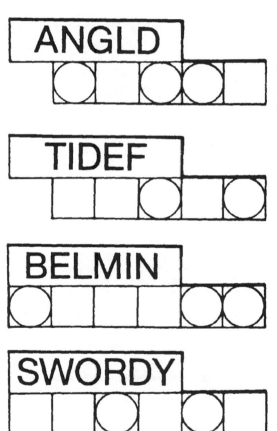

ANGLD

TIDEF

BELMIN

SWORDY

WHAT A PERSON WHO'S ALWAYS KICKING SELDOM HAS.

Now arrange the circled letters to form the surprise answer, as suggested by the above cartoon.

Print answer here A ⃝⃝⃝ TO ⃝⃝⃝⃝⃝⃝ ⃝⃝

JUMBLE®

Unscramble these four Jumbles, one letter to
each square, to form four ordinary words.

LOGUM

PUJEL

GREDIB

ONCOMM

Look at that idiot

IF A PEDESTRIAN
IS PRONE TO BE
CARELESS, HE MIGHT
END UP THIS WAY.

Now arrange the circled letters to form the
surprise answer, as suggested by the above
cartoon.

Print answer here

JUMBLE®

Unscramble these four Jumbles, one letter to each square, to form four ordinary words.

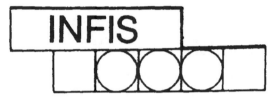

INFIS

LASIA

TANNIF

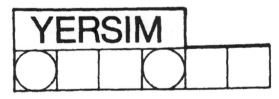

YERSIM

I took it off the shelf, dear

WHAT MANY AN AMATEUR GARDENER GETS FOR HIS PAINS.

Now arrange the circled letters to form the surprise answer, as suggested by the above cartoon.

Print answer here

JUMBLE®

Unscramble these four Jumbles, one letter to
each square, to form four ordinary words.

GYNAM

CAUMS

DYLOUB

THARGE

My rich uncle isn't
long for this world

A MAN WHO IS
ALWAYS ASKING FOR
A LOAN IS APT TO
BE LEFT THIS.

Now arrange the circled letters to form the
surprise answer, as suggested by the above
cartoon.

Print answer here

JUMBLE®

Unscramble these four Jumbles, one letter to
each square, to form four ordinary words.

LONEV

DAMAR

GOBNEY

MESECH

CREDIT MIGHT BE
THE MEANS TO
LIVE LIKE THIS.

Now arrange the circled letters to form the
surprise answer, as suggested by the above
cartoon.

**Print
answer
here** ◯◯◯◯◯◯ ONE'S ◯◯◯◯◯

JUMBLE®

Unscramble these four Jumbles, one letter to
each square, to form four ordinary words.

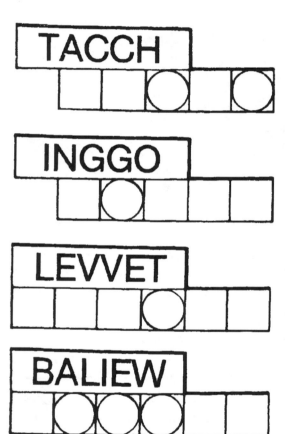

TACCH

INGGO

LEVVET

BALIEW

Sorry, Rodney

A DATE IS
SOMETHING YOU
MUST BREAK WHEN
YOU THIS.

Now arrange the circled letters to form the
surprise answer, as suggested by the above
cartoon.

Print answer here

JUMBLE®

Unscramble these four Jumbles, one letter to
each square, to form four ordinary words.

BATHI

PERAP

LARCIA

GURDIT

A YOUNG PERSON
MIGHT IMPROVE HIS
EYESIGHT WHEN HE
GETS THIS.

Now arrange the circled letters to form the
surprise answer, as suggested by the above
cartoon.

Print answer here

JUMBLE®

Unscramble these four Jumbles, one letter to each square, to form four ordinary words.

DATUL

SUGES

ORCEAN

SLUDON

Yes, dear, you're right as usual

WHAT HE SAID HIS WIFE'S REASONING LARGELY WAS.

Now arrange the circled letters to form the surprise answer, as suggested by the above cartoon.

Print answer here " ◯◯◯◯◯ "

JUMBLE®

Unscramble these four Jumbles, one letter to each square, to form four ordinary words.

SPEHE

VELGO

DYGOTS

GINDHI

Psst--
Why don't
you move
it?

I don't
think so

WHAT HIS HANDICAP
IN GOLF WAS.

Now arrange the circled letters to form the surprise answer, as suggested by the above cartoon.

Print answer here

JUMBLE®

Unscramble these four Jumbles, one letter to
each square, to form four ordinary words.

ELTAM

RACCK

ARIVED

TEKLET

THERE WAS A LOT OF
THIS IN THE WAITING
ROOM OF THE
EMPLOYMENT AGENCY.

Now arrange the circled letters to form the
surprise answer, as suggested by the above
cartoon.

Print answer here " ⬡⬡⬡⬡ " ⬡⬡⬡⬡

JUMBLE®

Unscramble these four Jumbles, one letter to each square, to form four ordinary words.

TAMID

CANYF

SLIMAD

GURTED

Welcome, to our new lifetime member

WHAT THE LAWYER WHO JOINED THE NUDIST COLONY NEVER HAD.

Now arrange the circled letters to form the surprise answer, as suggested by the above cartoon.

Print answer here A "◯◯◯◯◯" ◯◯◯◯◯◯

JUMBLE®

Unscramble these four Jumbles, one letter to each square, to form four ordinary words.

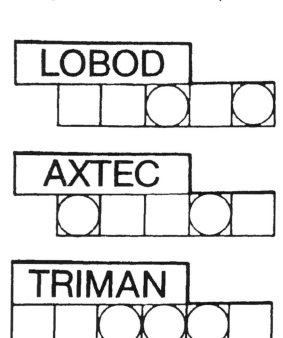

LOBOD

AXTEC

TRIMAN

GARUJA

He never listens to me!

A BOXER WHO FAILS TO CARRY OUT HIS SECOND'S SUGGESTIONS IS SOMETIMES THIS.

Now arrange the circled letters to form the surprise answer, as suggested by the above cartoon.

Print answer here

JUMBLE®

Unscramble these four Jumbles, one letter to
each square, to form four ordinary words.

YIXTS

BABIR

SAILEY

LEARNY

ONE IS NOT AT
LIBERTY TO TAKE
THIS WITH OTHERS.

Now arrange the circled letters to form the
surprise answer, as suggested by the above
cartoon.

Print answer here

JUMBLE®

Unscramble these four Jumbles, one letter to each square, to form four ordinary words.

SYNIO
⬜⬜⬜⬜⬜

BLEER
⬜⬜⬜⬜⬜

ADUMAR
⬜⬜⬜⬜⬜⬜

QULLAS
⬜⬜⬜⬜⬜⬜

WHAT THE BODYBUILDER-TURNED-CLAM DIGGER SEEMED TO BE.

Now arrange the circled letters to form the surprise answer, as suggested by the above cartoon.

Print answer here " ⬜⬜⬜⬜⬜⬜⬜ " – ⬜⬜⬜⬜⬜⬜

JUMBLE®

Unscramble these four Jumbles, one letter to each square, to form four ordinary words.

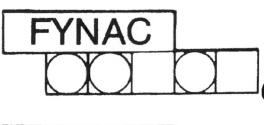

FYNAC

TENFO

LENZOZ

ARIDAL

WHAT THAT TIRESOME SPEECHMAKER COULD NOT BE AFTER HE WAS CALLED ON.

Now arrange the circled letters to form the surprise answer, as suggested by the above cartoon.

Print answer here

JUMBLE®

Unscramble these four Jumbles, one letter to each square, to form four ordinary words.

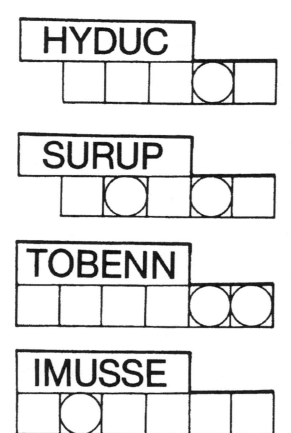

HYDUC

SURUP

TOBENN

IMUSSE

Wouldn't hurt if you both lost a few pounds

HIS WORST FAULT IS TELLING OTHER PEOPLE—

Now arrange the circled letters to form the surprise answer, as suggested by the above cartoon.

Print answer here

JUMBLE®

Unscramble these four Jumbles, one letter to each square, to form four ordinary words.

LAIGE

ARVEG

CHABRE

NENFLE

MATERNITY

Wow! I'm a dad!

WHAT A BRAND-NEW FATHER IS ABOUT TO ENTER INTO.

Now arrange the circled letters to form the surprise answer, as suggested by the above cartoon.

Print answer here A ⬡⬡⬡⬡⬡⬡⬡⬡ WORLD

JUMBLE®

Unscramble these four Jumbles, one letter to each square, to form four ordinary words.

ATLAN
◯◯◯□□

KISLY
◯◯◯□□

NACUNE
□□◯□□◯

HERDIT
◯◯□◯□□

After you, J.B.

His father owns the company

USED TO OPEN DOORS IN THE BUSINESS WORLD.

Now arrange the circled letters to form the surprise answer, as suggested by the above cartoon.

Print answer here ◯◯◯◯◯◯◯

JUMBLE®

Unscramble these four Jumbles, one letter to each square, to form four ordinary words.

TRAAL

SOITH

FRYLUR

EPALUG

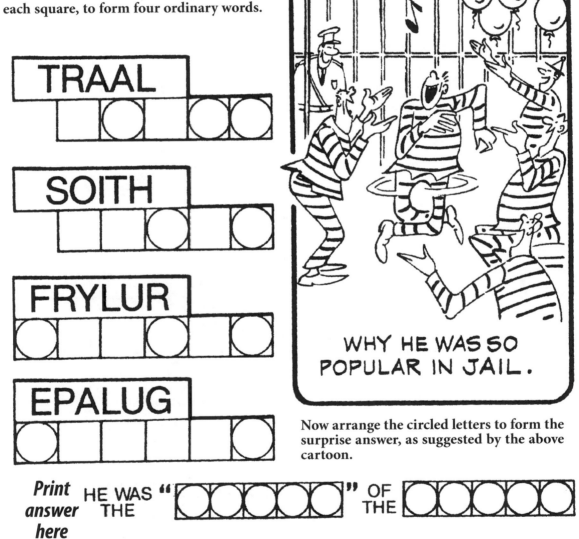

WHY HE WAS SO POPULAR IN JAIL.

Now arrange the circled letters to form the surprise answer, as suggested by the above cartoon.

Print answer here HE WAS " ⬡⬡⬡⬡⬡ " OF THE ⬡⬡⬡⬡⬡

JUMBLE®

Unscramble these four Jumbles, one letter to each square, to form four ordinary words.

DUXEE

CARPH

LARCOR

NARFIA

AN OUTFIT THAT MAKES ONE WOMAN LOOK SLIM OFTEN MAKES OTHERS LOOK THIS.

Now arrange the circled letters to form the surprise answer, as suggested by the above cartoon.

Print answer here " ◯◯◯◯◯ "

JUMBLE®

Unscramble these four Jumbles, one letter to
each square, to form four ordinary words.

ASTEE

LAHCK

SCEXIE

REDDEG

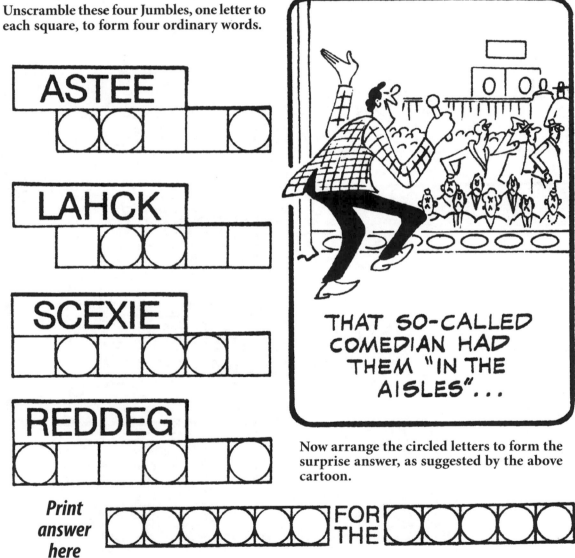

THAT SO-CALLED
COMEDIAN HAD
THEM "IN THE
AISLES"...

Now arrange the circled letters to form the
surprise answer, as suggested by the above
cartoon.

**Print
answer
here**

☐☐☐☐☐☐ FOR
THE ☐☐☐☐☐

JUMBLE®

Unscramble these four Jumbles, one letter to each square, to form four ordinary words.

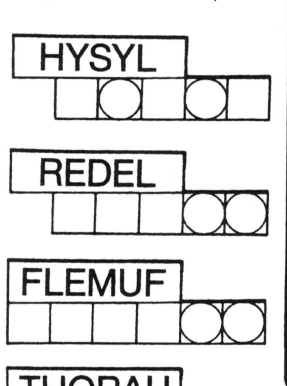

HYSYL

REDEL

FLEMUF

THORAU

THEY SAID SHE WAS BEAUTIFUL BUT NOT QUITE THIS.

Now arrange the circled letters to form the surprise answer, as suggested by the above cartoon.

Print answer here "◯◯◯ ◯◯◯◯◯"

JUMBLE®

Unscramble these four Jumbles, one letter to
each square, to form four ordinary words.

NIKKY

MAGLE

SVALIE

LAIWHE

He shouldn't be
gossiping like that

ONE WAY TO KEEP
FRIENDS IS NOT
TO DO THIS.

Now arrange the circled letters to form the
surprise answer, as suggested by the above
cartoon.

Print answer here " ⬡⬡⬡⬡⬡ THEM ⬡⬡⬡⬡ "

JUMBLE®

Unscramble these four Jumbles, one letter to
each square, to form four ordinary words.

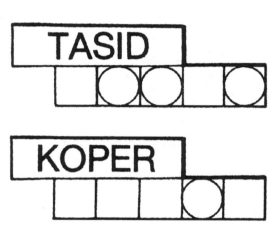

TASID

KOPER

FLENNE

POATTE

PEOPLE WHO TRAVEL
IN ORDER TO
BECOME BROADENED
SOMETIMES RETURN
HOME THIS WAY.

Now arrange the circled letters to form the
surprise answer, as suggested by the above
cartoon.

Print answer here " ◯◯◯◯◯◯◯◯◯◯ "

JUMBLE®

Unscramble these four Jumbles, one letter to each square, to form four ordinary words.

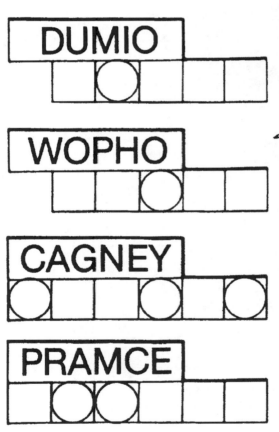

DUMIO

WOPHO

CAGNEY

PRAMCE

WHAT THE FIRST DAY OF THE WEEK CAN BE.

Now arrange the circled letters to form the surprise answer, as suggested by the above cartoon.

Print answer here "  "

JUMBLE®

Unscramble these four Jumbles, one letter to each square, to form four ordinary words.

SOGOE

KLEAN

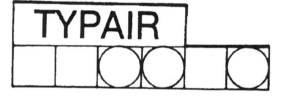

TYPAIR

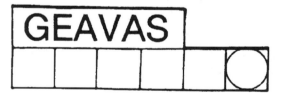

GEAVAS

WHAT THEIR BABIES' BEDROOM WAS CALLED.

Now arrange the circled letters to form the surprise answer, as suggested by the above cartoon.

Print answer here THE " ⬡⬡⬡⬡⬡⬡⬡ "

JUMBLE®

Unscramble these four Jumbles, one letter to each square, to form four ordinary words.

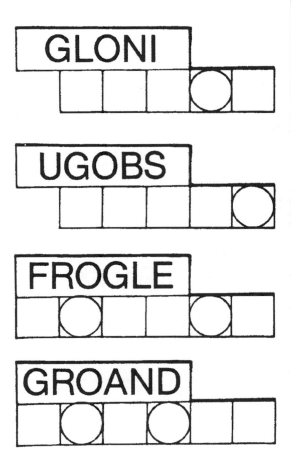

GLONI

UGOBS

FROGLE

GROAND

WHAT THEY SAID
WHEN THEY SAW
THE GRAND CANYON.

Now arrange the circled letters to form the surprise answer, as suggested by the above cartoon.

Print answer here "  "

JUMBLE®

Unscramble these four Jumbles, one letter to
each square, to form four ordinary words.

TYSUL

YOANG

SPYGUM

PERRAY

KEEPING UP WITH
THE JONESES
MIGHT ALSO
INVOLVE KEEPING
UP WITH THESE.

Now arrange the circled letters to form the
surprise answer, as suggested by the above
cartoon.

Print answer here THE

JUMBLE®

Unscramble these four Jumbles, one letter to each square, to form four ordinary words.

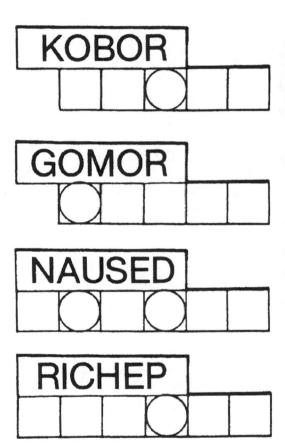

KOBOR

GOMOR

NAUSED

RICHEP

Ugh!

WHAT THOSE SOCIETY "CRUMBS" WERE HELD TOGETHER BY.

Now arrange the circled letters to form the surprise answer, as suggested by the above cartoon.

Print answer here "  "

JUMBLE®

Unscramble these four Jumbles, one letter to each square, to form four ordinary words.

NISHY

JECET

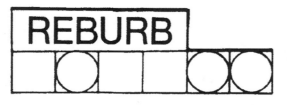

REBURB

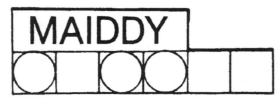

MAIDDY

Too bad he wasn't a nicer person

WHAT THE BILLIONAIRE LEFT WHEN HE DIED.

Now arrange the circled letters to form the surprise answer, as suggested by the above cartoon.

Print answer here

TO BE

JUMBLE®

Unscramble these four Jumbles, one letter to each square, to form four ordinary words.

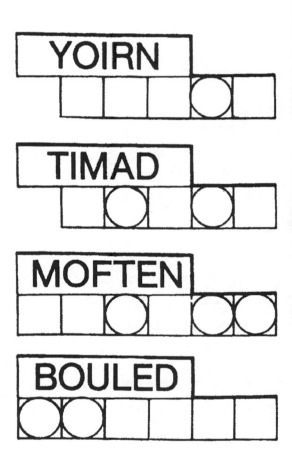

YOIRN

TIMAD

MOFTEN

BOULED

Our little dolls

PERMISSIVE PARENTS DON'T MIND WHEN THEIR KIDS THIS.

Now arrange the circled letters to form the surprise answer, as suggested by the above cartoon.

Print answer here ⬡⬡⬡'⬡ ⬡⬡⬡⬡⬡

151

JUMBLE®

Unscramble these four Jumbles, one letter to each square, to form four ordinary words.

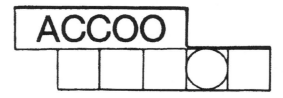

ACCOO

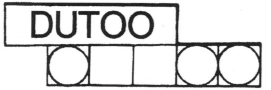

DUTOO

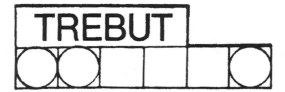

TREBUT

ENTHIZ

You've had enough!

HE DOESN'T LIKE TO BE ORDERED AROUND UNLESS IT'S THIS.

Now arrange the circled letters to form the surprise answer, as suggested by the above cartoon.

Print answer here A ⬡⬡⬡⬡⬡ OF ⬡⬡⬡⬡⬡

JUMBLE®

Unscramble these four Jumbles, one letter to each square, to form four ordinary words.

GORRI

AMGUT

LOCASE

INTOAR

WHAT SHE WISHED HER ADMIRERS WOULD PRACTICE.

Now arrange the circled letters to form the surprise answer, as suggested by the above cartoon.

Print answer here " ⬡⬡⬡⬡ " ⬡⬡⬡⬡⬡⬡⬡⬡

JUMBLE®

Unscramble these four Jumbles, one letter to
each square, to form four ordinary words.

RIGMY

TRUPE

DELAUF

STERJE

Those were the good old days when I controlled all that money

You'll have some special privileges here

WHAT AN
UNETHICAL TRUSTEE
SOMETIMES
ENDS UP AS.

Now arrange the circled letters to form the
surprise answer, as suggested by the above
cartoon.

Print answer here

154

JUMBLE®

Unscramble these four Jumbles, one letter to each square, to form four ordinary words.

LUFAW

RAPPE

STAJEM

HERNID

I don't know what he's got to be snooty about

WHAT NEPOTISM MEANS IN THE FIELD OF EMPLOYMENT.

Now arrange the circled letters to form the surprise answer, as suggested by the above cartoon.

Print answer here TO ◯◯◯ ON "◯◯◯◯◯"

JUMBLE®

Unscramble these four Jumbles, one letter to
each square, to form four ordinary words.

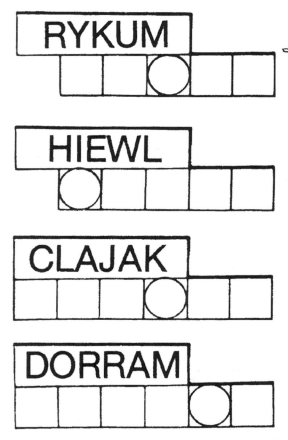

RYKUM

HIEWL

CLAJAK

DORRAM

A FOUR - LETTER
WORD THAT SOME
PEOPLE FIND MOST
"OBJECTIONABLE."

Now arrange the circled letters to form the
surprise answer, as suggested by the above
cartoon.

Print answer here "  "

JUMBLE®

Unscramble these four Jumbles, one letter to each square, to form four ordinary words.

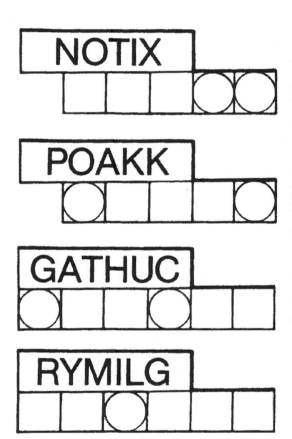

NOTIX

POAKK

GATHUC

RYMILG

We want our money back

SOMETIMES WHEN THE PLAYERS DO THE RUNNING, THE FANS DO THIS.

Now arrange the circled letters to form the surprise answer, as suggested by the above cartoon.

Print answer here THE ⬡⬡⬡⬡⬡⬡⬡⬡

JUMBLE®

Unscramble these four Jumbles, one letter to each square, to form four ordinary words.

SASIB

ECTAN

TABBIR

FATOLA

WHAT SOME PARENTS EXPERIENCE WHEN THEY HAVE TEENAGE KIDS.

Now arrange the circled letters to form the surprise answer, as suggested by the above cartoon.

Print answer here " ◯◯◯◯◯◯◯◯◯◯ "

JUMBLE®

Unscramble these four Jumbles, one letter to
each square, to form four ordinary words.

DYLAL

EVVER

YETHIG

TEENAB

Some family!

But no worse than most others

WHAT MANY FAMILY PROBLEMS ARE.

Now arrange the circled letters to form the
surprise answer, as suggested by the above
cartoon.

Print answer here ALL " ◯◯◯◯◯◯◯◯ "

JUMBLE®

Unscramble these four Jumbles, one letter to each square, to form four ordinary words.

YOHEN

VARAL

LAWTUN

DIMROB

IF HE STARTS RIGHT OUT COMPLAINING ABOUT HER COOKING, SHE'LL LEARN BETTER...

Now arrange the circled letters to form the surprise answer, as suggested by the above cartoon.

Print answer here

JUMBLE®

Unscramble these four Jumbles, one letter to
each square, to form four ordinary words.

YIEPT

DRIAP

PADIUN

TULYSS

HOW MANY A
"CHECKERED"
CAREER ENDS UP.

Now arrange the circled letters to form the
surprise answer, as suggested by the above
cartoon.

**Print
answer
here** IN A ☐☐☐☐☐☐☐ ☐☐☐☐

JUMBLE®

Unscramble these four Jumbles, one letter to each square, to form four ordinary words.

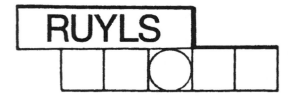

RUYLS

NYPOH

STYJUL

TRALFE

Wonder how he makes his living

A lot of people found out—to their sorrow

ANY MAN WHO SURVIVES BY "DOING NOTHING" IS PROBABLY REALLY DOING THIS.

Now arrange the circled letters to form the surprise answer, as suggested by the above cartoon.

Print answer here

Jumpin'
JUMBLE®

Challenger Puzzles

JUMBLE®

Unscramble these six Jumbles, one letter to each square, to form six ordinary words.

NITTEK

RODIAH

TIPURY

VAHLIS

LOCSRL

MOSHNA

Cedar is the best

I just did a den in maple

WHEN THE CAR-
PENTERS GOT
TOGETHER, THEY
HAD A—

Now arrange the circled letters to form the surprise answer, as suggested by the above cartoon.

PRINT YOUR ANSWER IN THE CIRCLES BELOW

JUMBLE.

Unscramble these six Jumbles, one letter to
each square, to form six ordinary words.

INGRYT

FEWLOU

NAVCAT

TENNIT

GEDUBB

TAIXLY

This place
is awful

But close to
the port

WHAT THE SUB-
MARINE CREW
DID ON SHORE
LEAVE.

Now arrange the circled letters to form the
surprise answer, as suggested by the above
cartoon.

PRINT YOUR ANSWER IN THE CIRCLES BELOW

JUMBLE®

Unscramble these six Jumbles, one letter to each square, to form six ordinary words.

PRAUPE

YALSAW

ROHTAU

CRANDI

TOALZE

HUMILE

We're broke

No more charging

WHEN THE NURSE WENT OVER BUDGET, HER CREDIT CARDS BECAME THIS.

Now arrange the circled letters to form the surprise answer, as suggested by the above cartoon.

PRINT YOUR ANSWER IN THE CIRCLES BELOW

A ◯◯◯◯◯◯◯ ◯◯◯◯◯◯

JUMBLE

Unscramble these six Jumbles, one letter to
each square, to form six ordinary words.

GUNSLY

CLARNE

GINKAB

BLOGIE

VEWERS

NUIRJY

BULLETIN: We interrupt this program...

Danny broke
a dish

MOM WAS
GREETED WITH
THIS WHEN SHE
CAME HOME.

Now arrange the circled letters to form the
surprise answer, as suggested by the above
cartoon.

PRINT YOUR ANSWER IN THE CIRCLES BELOW

" ◯◯◯◯◯◯◯◯ " ◯◯◯◯

JUMBLE®

Unscramble these six Jumbles, one letter to each square, to form six ordinary words.

TYKONT

FLUNGE

LARMON

LAAXYG

INROUJ

ENMUIM

What's next?

What did you read?

WHAT THE INSTRUCTION BOOK GAVE THE PLUMBER'S APPRENTICE.

Now arrange the circled letters to form the surprise answer, as suggested by the above cartoon.

PRINT YOUR ANSWER IN THE CIRCLES BELOW

" ⬡⬡⬡⬡⬡⬡ " ⬡⬡⬡⬡⬡⬡⬡⬡

JUMBLE®

Unscramble these six Jumbles, one letter to
each square, to form six ordinary words.

ZELZUG

REVOND

WELLOB

KLACEY

SHMAIF

DENEEL

DING
DONG
DING
DON

ANOTHER NAME
FOR BRIDESMAIDS
IN THE OLD
SOUTH.

Now arrange the circled letters to form the
surprise answer, as suggested by the above
cartoon.

PRINT YOUR ANSWER IN THE CIRCLES BELOW

JUMBLE®

Unscramble these six Jumbles, one letter to each square, to form six ordinary words.

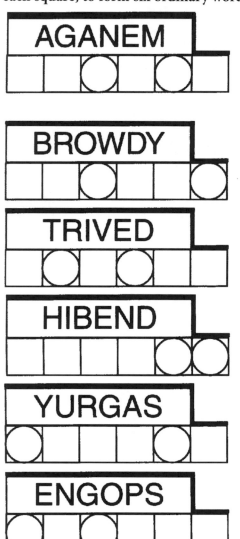

AGANEM

BROWDY

TRIVED

HIBEND

YURGAS

ENGOPS

That's your idea of being all dressed up?

WHAT MOM GAVE JUNIOR WHEN SHE SAW HIS OUTFIT.

Now arrange the circled letters to form the surprise answer, as suggested by the above cartoon.

PRINT YOUR ANSWER IN THE CIRCLES BELOW

A ⬡⬡⬡⬡⬡⬡⬡⬡ ⬡⬡⬡⬡

JUMBLE®

Unscramble these six Jumbles, one letter to each square, to form six ordinary words.

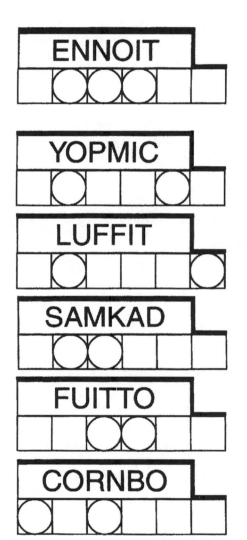

ENNOIT

YOPMIC

LUFFIT

SAMKAD

FUITTO

CORNBO

Good job. You're going places

I can do a lot more

NEEDED TO GET THE HAY IN THE BARN.

Now arrange the circled letters to form the surprise answer, as suggested by the above cartoon.

PRINT YOUR ANSWER IN THE CIRCLES BELOW

A " ☐☐☐☐ - ☐ " ☐☐☐☐☐☐☐☐☐

JUMBLE®

Unscramble these six Jumbles, one letter to each square, to form six ordinary words.

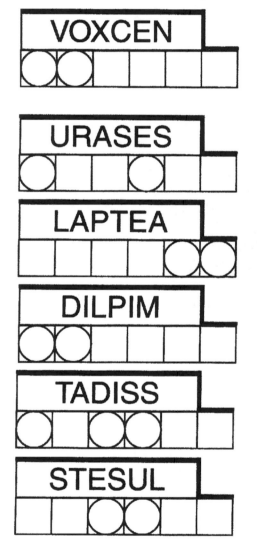

VOXCEN

URASES

LAPTEA

DILPIM

TADISS

STESUL

She comes from the wrong side of the tracks — Hortense knows everybody

HOW BLUE-BLOOD MATRONS KNOW WHO IS WHO.

Now arrange the circled letters to form the surprise answer, as suggested by the above cartoon.

PRINT YOUR ANSWER IN THE CIRCLES BELOW

JUMBLE®

Unscramble these six Jumbles, one letter to each square, to form six ordinary words.

EUMMUS

CHENUQ

GRAVEA

CEEDDO

YASUNE

CLINPE

What's the guarantee?

WHAT THE MAGI-
CIAN LOOKED
FOR IN HIS
CONTRACT.

Now arrange the circled letters to form the surprise answer, as suggested by the above cartoon.

PRINT YOUR ANSWER IN THE CIRCLES BELOW

AN " ⬡⬡⬡⬡⬡⬡ " ⬡⬡⬡⬡⬡⬡

JUMBLE®

Unscramble these six Jumbles, one letter to
each square, to form six ordinary words.

DURSTY

COYPIL

GHURNY

RICOTE

PERMAC

DRIPEM

All fresh. Picked
them today

A SUCCESSFUL
VEGETABLE
FARMER
WILL DO THIS.

Now arrange the circled letters to form the
surprise answer, as suggested by the above
cartoon.

PRINT YOUR ANSWER IN THE CIRCLES BELOW

JUMBLE®

Unscramble these six Jumbles, one letter to
each square, to form six ordinary words.

NEUQUI

ANNEMP

PAKRUM

BRAKEM

CIPTED

TEYQUI

We have to
get down

Not
now—
We're so
close

WHAT THE CLIMBER
EXPERIENCED
WHEN HE
COULDN'T REACH
THE SUMMIT.

Now arrange the circled letters to form the
surprise answer, as suggested by the above
cartoon.

PRINT YOUR ANSWER IN THE CIRCLES BELOW

A

JUMBLE®

Unscramble these six Jumbles, one letter to each square, to form six ordinary words.

NORREC

LEESAW

PURBAT

YUPRIF

LYKING

SARGYS

This is it. From now on I'll use cash

WHAT THE DOC-
TOR RESORTED
TO WHEN THE
CREDIT CHARGES
GOT TOO HIGH.

Now arrange the circled letters to form the surprise answer, as suggested by the above cartoon.

PRINT YOUR ANSWER IN THE CIRCLES BELOW

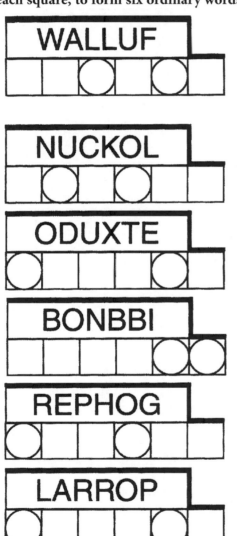

JUMBLE®

Unscramble these six Jumbles, one letter to
each square, to form six ordinary words.

WALLUF

NUCKOL

ODUXTE

BONBBI

REPHOG

LARROP

Just a little bit
higher...no, lower

THE TAILOR HAD
TROUBLE WITH
THE WRESTLER
BECAUSE HE
WAS—

Now arrange the circled letters to form the
surprise answer, as suggested by the above
cartoon.

PRINT YOUR ANSWER IN THE CIRCLES BELOW

TO

JUMBLE®

Unscramble these six Jumbles, one letter to each square, to form six ordinary words.

CAMBEL

REGOUM

HAWLIE

SCARFA

PRAILL

GONBEE

He never stops talking

THE VENTRILO-QUIST SAID HIS DUMMY WAS THIS.

Now arrange the circled letters to form the surprise answer, as suggested by the above cartoon.

PRINT YOUR ANSWER IN THE CIRCLES BELOW

A ⬡⬡⬡⬡⬡⬡ OF " ⬡⬡⬡⬡⬡⬡ "

JUMBLE®

Unscramble these six Jumbles, one letter to each square, to form six ordinary words.

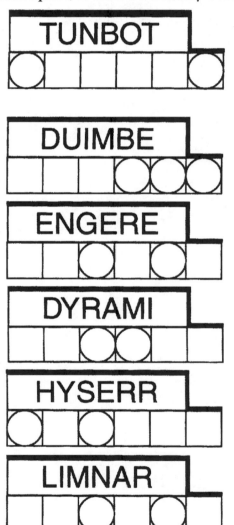

TUNBOT

DUIMBE

ENGERE

DYRAMI

HYSERR

LIMNAR

No phones, no reports, hot sun, nice tan

THE OFFICE WORKER YEARNED FOR A DAY AT THE BEACH BECAUSE SHE HAD—

Now arrange the circled letters to form the surprise answer, as suggested by the above cartoon.

PRINT YOUR ANSWER IN THE CIRCLES BELOW

A " ◯◯◯◯◯◯◯ " ◯◯◯◯◯◯

JUMBLE®

Unscramble these six Jumbles, one letter to
each square, to form six ordinary words.

UNMEBB

NURTUE

ENTHIZ

ROMMIE

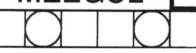

MEEGUL

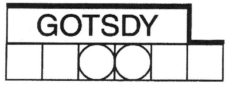

GOTSDY

How come
I get all
the work?

OK, give me
some from
your pile

HOW DID THE
TAILORS SETTLE
THEIR DIFFER-
ENCES?

Now arrange the circled letters to form the
surprise answer, as suggested by the above
cartoon.

PRINT YOUR ANSWER IN THE CIRCLES BELOW

JUMBLE®

Unscramble these six Jumbles, one letter to each square, to form six ordinary words.

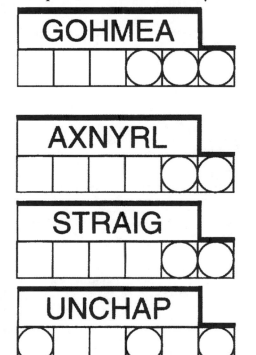

GOHMEA

AXNYRL

STRAIG

UNCHAP

BEFILE

WIMDLE

Gosh, Mom, you sure make it sparkle

WHAT MOM BECAME WHEN SHE POLISHED THE SILVERWARE.

Now arrange the circled letters to form the surprise answer, as suggested by the above cartoon.

PRINT YOUR ANSWER IN THE CIRCLES BELOW

A "◯◯◯◯◯◯◯" ◯◯◯◯◯◯◯

JUMBLE®

Unscramble these six Jumbles, one letter to
each square, to form six ordinary words.

YOMPLE

EXGONY

NORIPS

HURGOT

PLECOM

LEFTLI

How do I
love thee ...

The words
are so
beautiful

WHEN HIS PROSE
BROUGHT TEARS
TO HER EYES, SHE
SAID IT WAS—

Now arrange the circled letters to form the
surprise answer, as suggested by the above
cartoon.

PRINT YOUR ANSWER IN THE CIRCLES BELOW

JUMBLE

Unscramble these six Jumbles, one letter to
each square, to form six ordinary words.

BLIMEN

CILTIA

TYMINE

SIDEME

RULTSY

TEENIC

Gee, officer, I
must have left my
license at home

WHAT THE PSYCHI-
ATRIST FACED
WHEN HE WAS
STOPPED FOR
SPEEDING.

Now arrange the circled letters to form the
surprise answer, as suggested by the above
cartoon.

PRINT YOUR ANSWER IN THE CIRCLES BELOW

AN

ANSWERS

1. **Jumbles:** KITTY LEAVE BAKERY MAGNET
   Answer: Where the opera singer's little aria came from—A BIG "AREA"

2. **Jumbles:** CATCH LYING GENIUS VANISH
   Answer: What there was plenty of at that penthouse—HIGH LIVING

3. **Jumbles:** WEIGH BEGUN PLENTY BUREAU
   Answer: How some frank people make their point—BY BEING BLUNT

4. **Jumbles:** DOUBT KNOWN EXCITE JOVIAL
   Answer: What the bus driver said—"JACK," IN THE BOX

5. **Jumbles:** WOMEN PECAN HALVED GUTTER
   Answer: What those talkative moths did—CHEWED THE RAG

6. **Jumbles:** RAINY CUBIT LOCATE DOUBLY
   Answer: Tired of looking at all those roadside ads—"BILL-BORED"

7. **Jumbles:** PARKA TOXIC DROPSY ACCORD
   Answer: What a person who spends every afternoon watching TV undoubtedly is—A "SOAP" ADDICT

8. **Jumbles:** QUILT GORGE SHAKEN BLOUSE
   Answer: Why they always accused him of being negative—HE WAS A "NO-IT-ALL"

9. **Jumbles:** LIMBO BRAWL FUTURE PYTHON
   Answer: When it comes to a dishwasher, most every husband would rather do this—BUY THAN BE

10. **Jumbles:** BANJO PROVE DIVIDE ZENITH
    Answer: What the hula dancer did to the guys in the audience—"HIP-NOTIZED" 'EM

11. **Jumbles:** MIDGE NUTTY CRAYON BUSHEL
    Answer: What her steady date was much of the time—UNSTEADY

12. **Jumbles:** COVEY DIZZY KNIGHT HAZARD
    Answer: What all that talk about horoscopes was—"ZODI-YAK"

13. **Jumbles:** VITAL LOOSE SCHOOL TARTAR
    Answer: What the discount real estate broker offered to sell—"LOTS" FOR LITTLE

14. **Jumbles:** TUNED NUDGE BOILED POTTER
    Answer: That door-to-door salesman got only one order—"GET OUT!"

15. **Jumbles:** BATON NOISE DAWNED HARDLY
    Answer: Why they called her a suicide blonde—"DYED" BY HER OWN HAND

16. **Jumbles:** OUNCE ABHOR FELONY NAUSEA
    Answer: He laughed up his sleeve because that's where this was—HIS FUNNY BONE

17. **Jumbles:** BLESS WHEEL LAYOFF SEETHE
    Answer: Why business is always good for the vendor of peanuts—THEY "SHELL" FAST

18. **Jumbles:** FABLE MONEY HERESY SHEKEL
    Answer: What a foot doctor sometimes does—HEALS "HEELS"

19. **Jumbles:** MINCE EXPEL ANEMIA WIDEST
    Answer: A counterfeiter is the only man in the world who makes more money than this—ANYONE CAN SPEND

20. **Jumbles:** CHIME GLAND FALLEN BEAVER
    Answer: Jealousy sets in with the arrival of this—A RIVAL

21. **Jumbles:** GNOME SHAKY CLAUSE DECEIT
    Answer: The "go-getter" knows that the rules for getting ahead won't work unless this happens—HE DOES

22. **Jumbles:** SNOWY EMERY DETAIN GOITER
    Answer: What the globetrotter had—A "ROAMIN'" NOSE

23. **Jumbles:** CURRY PIOUS DECADE SALUTE
    Answer: How careless drivers frequently end up—"CARLESS"

24. **Jumbles:** BATCH ELATE DELUGE CURFEW
    Answer: What that "go-getter" finally managed to do—"GET HER"

25. **Jumbles:** FLUID HOUSE OPPOSE SQUALL
    Answer: What the female dinosaur said to her grouchy mate—YOU OLD FOSSIL

26. **Jumbles:** TWINE NAÏVE EYELET MISUSE
    Answer: The crowd did this when the winning team passed by—LET OFF "ESTEEM"

27. **Jumbles:** VIRUS FINAL HANSOM UNSAID
    Answer: What the city required in order to clean up the aftermath of a big snowstorm—A "SLUSH" FUND

28. **Jumbles:** HUMID PIPER ENTITY MYSELF
    Answer: Fat is the penalty for exceeding this—THE FEED LIMIT

29. **Jumbles:** PIKER ADULT MUSEUM PURVEY
    Answer: What they called that great magician—A SUPER "DUPER"

30. **Jumbles:** PARCH CHASM BAZAAR HELIUM
    Answer: Another name for rabbit fur—HARE HAIR

31. **Jumbles:** PEACE ROACH WINNOW MARLIN
    Answer: They used to consider him a "rake," but now he's simply turned into this—A LAWN MOWER

32. **Jumbles:** YACHT MURKY UNLIKE FORGER
    Answer: He built a good fire, and she said this—"GRATE-FUL!"

33. **Jumbles:** WOVEN SHAKY OCELOT HOOKUP
    Answer: The boxing ring is no place for this—A SLOW "POKE"

34. **Jumbles:** DECAY QUEEN FLORID ELIXIR
    Answer: What the stag did when the hunters arrived—RAN FOR "DEER" LIFE

35. **Jumbles:** ABOVE FLAME CALICO ENZYME
    Answer: What the big dairy farmer had lots of—"MOO-LA"

36. **Jumbles:** DOWDY FAULT GLOBAL POISON
    Answer: What she proceeded to do after her boyfriend canceled their date—BLOW HER TOP

37. **Jumbles:** SLANT MERGE RAREFY ZODIAC
    Answer: Another name for nostalgia—"YESTERDAZE"

38. **Jumbles:** AWOKE PILOT VORTEX DENOTE
    Answer: He couldn't swim a stroke, but he knew this—EVERY "DIVE" IN TOWN

39. **Jumbles:** PIECE SANDY KINGLY ENCAMP
    Answer: Their kid's college education seemed to be just this—PIGSKIN DEEP

40. **Jumbles:** LINEN ANNUL ENCORE HANSOM
    Answer: What that blackguard was—A HEEL WITHOUT A "SOLE"

41. **Jumbles:** TWINE CHICK INFIRM BEHELD
    Answer: She went to some length to change this—HER WIDTH

42. **Jumbles:** AFIRE PIANO ZIGZAG FOMENT
    Answer: Like a ship, some speakers toot loudest when they're this—IN A FOG

43. **Jumbles:** WINCE MUSIC RARITY INDOOR
    Answer: A politician is a man who's sworn into office and then this afterward—SWORN AT

44. **Jumbles:** HASTY CHAIR TUMULT STOLID
    Answer: You can lose weight best by not talking about it, but by keeping this—YOUR MOUTH SHUT

45. **Jumbles:** QUIRE DADDY FLURRY CENSUS
    Answer: A young man who spends too much time sowing his wild oats might begin to look this—"SEEDY"

46. **Jumbles:** FOLIO IRATE VIRTUE WHOLLY
Answer: A family that lives within its income usually has to learn to do this—LIVE WITHOUT

47. **Jumbles:** LISLE ADAGE JABBER BLOODY
Answer: What the ophthalmologists called their annual shindig—THE "EYE BALL"

48. **Jumbles:** KNELL GAWKY NORMAL DEBATE
Answer: That engaged couple was on the verge of breaking up before she finally managed to do this—BREAK HIM DOWN

49. **Jumbles:** PANIC LOOSE CHALET UNHOOK
Answer: What cap is never removed?—THE KNEECAP

50. **Jumbles:** ENTRY BRINY DRUDGE HANDLE
Answer: What the formerly "heavy" client at the reducing salon said after she lost all that weight—"DE-LIGHT-ED"

51. **Jumbles:** OZONE CHEEK INDUCT MILDEW
Answer: What the pillow tycoon got when business was bad—"DOWN" IN THE MOUTH

52. **Jumbles:** BANAL NOTCH SPORTY TRAGIC
Answer: When prices on everything else went up at that store, envelopes remained this—"STATIONARY" (stationery)

53. **Jumbles:** CRAZY DANDY KOWTOW HALVED
Answer: He spent his money like water but not this—ON WATER

54. **Jumbles:** TOOTH BLOAT LEGUME SCORCH
Answer: Where grave robbers learn their profession—IN GHOUL SCHOOL

55. **Jumbles:** VITAL WHEAT FOSSIL RENDER
Answer: What an airline might do in order to drum up business—HAND OUT "FLIERS"

56. **Jumbles:** NOBLE DAILY FRIEZE CATNIP
Answer: What happens when two egotists have a falling out—IT'S AN "I" FOR AN "I"

57. **Jumbles:** MOUSE AVAIL VOYAGE NAUSEA
Answer: She's determined to do this, no matter how much it costs—SAVE MONEY

58. **Jumbles:** SURLY ENSUE LEGACY PARISH
Answer: What did they call the team made up of Frankenstein monsters?—THE "ALL-SCARS"

59. **Jumbles:** ESSAY AZURE TOUCHY LEDGER
Answer: He makes a monkey of himself whenever he tries to do this—CARRY A "TALE"

60. **Jumbles:** EMPTY AROMA PENCIL SMOKER
Answer: Why the worms didn't enter Noah's ark in "pairs"—THEY CAME IN APPLES

61. **Jumbles:** LEGAL MOOSE RAREFY HICCUP
Answer: Praise this and you're sure to turn a woman's head—HER PROFILE

62. **Jumbles:** LOONY FOUNT ORPHAN GUITAR
Answer: Why they found the nudist camp so boring—NOTHING WENT ON

63. **Jumbles:** HOARD SKULL UPTOWN FLORID
Answer: How the manicurist rejected his proposal of marriage—OUT OF HAND

64. **Jumbles:** FINAL DERBY NUANCE HOURLY
Answer: Another name for a dialogue—A DOUBLE "CHIN"

65. **Jumbles:** AGENT EIGHT GENTRY MORBID
Answer: She was always sure to keep a secret…GOING

66. **Jumbles:** AHEAD CABIN FIASCO IMPEND
Answer: Apparently it's a sign of good manners to put up with this—BAD ONES

67. **Jumbles:** HENCE SNACK EMBARK COWARD
Answer: "When did you first notice that weak back?"—"A WEEK BACK"

68. **Jumbles:** ROUSE FAMED GROUCH DONKEY
Answer: The baker left his job because he didn't this—"KNEAD" THE DOUGH

69. **Jumbles:** DIRTY BAGGY GUIDED ANSWER
Answer: What do you get when a fat man marries a fat lady?—A BIG WEDDING

70. **Jumbles:** LEECH JUROR MOTIVE BELFRY
Answer: What you might expect him to do when she spends all that money on some silly art object—OBJECT

71. **Jumbles:** POISE HITCH DEMISE EYEFUL
Answer: What's a mermaid?—A "DEEP-SHE FISH"

72. **Jumbles:** HOIST APART STIGMA POTTER
Answer: What many a night spot is—A "TIGHT" SPOT

73. **Jumbles:** GRIEF PAUSE EROTIC COLUMN
Answer: You can't get rid of a bad temper by doing this—LOSING IT

74. **Jumbles:** HOUSE CRAWL OCCULT URCHIN
Answer: Another name for the time you spend going home from work—THE "CRUSH" HOUR

75. **Jumbles:** ADULT GLOVE FLABBY LEVITY
Answer: Add this on for your protection, if you're about to invest—"-IGATE"

76. **Jumbles:** BASSO WEARY RITUAL MASCOT
Answer: His clothes tell you a lot about this—HIS "WEAR"-ABOUTS

77. **Jumbles:** TRYST DUCAL BRIDLE HANGAR
Answer: He's old enough to know better but too old to do this—CARE

78. **Jumbles:** TULLE FUDGE PELVIS SUPERB
Answer: What a good insecticide might be—A "PEST" SELLER

79. **Jumbles:** SYNOD CAKED KETTLE ANYHOW
Answer: Every dog has its "day" except one with a sore tail, which has this—ITS "WEAK END"

80. **Jumbles:** RAVEN GUMBO LEVITY CUDGEL
Answer: How they knew that the man-eating shark had been shot dead—THERE WAS A "BULLET-IN"

81. **Jumbles:** TASTY PARKA OBLIGE DOUBLE
Answer: Why the shopkeeper said farewell to that bargain merchandise—IT WAS "A GOOD BUY"

82. **Jumbles:** UNCLE TOPAZ ORPHAN SOLACE
Answer: That dumbbell was planning to put his feet into the oven in order to do this—POP HIS CORNS

83. **Jumbles:** DUMPY HENCE RUBBER FORGET
Answer: The restaurant across from the theater was always packed because the play was strictly this—"FROM HUNGER"

84. **Jumbles:** BLOOM OFTEN ABSURD LEGUME
Answer: What kind of personality did that champion fencer have?—A "DUEL" ONE

85. **Jumbles:** FINAL MOOSE HEALTH FONDLY
Answer: What a man in love sometimes shows great ingenuity in making—A FOOL OF HIMSELF

86. **Jumbles:** BROOK DADDY ADROIT MEASLY
Answer: That beloved movie villain was so good at being this—SO BAD

87. **Jumbles:** CYNIC FAMED BARREL ABRUPT
Answer: How the backseat driver's husband drove—BY EAR

88. **Jumbles:** ASSAY LUNGE HINDER SPEEDY
Answer: Rich food, like destiny, can do this—SHAPE OUR ENDS

89. **Jumbles:** AGILE CABIN FESTAL COHORT
Answer: They named their team the Spiders because all of them knew how to do this—CATCH FLIES

90. **Jumbles:** AGENT HOBBY IMPUTE DROWSY
Answer: What that undercover agent was also known as—A SPY IN BED

91. **Jumbles:** ADMIT ROBIN STUCCO JUNGLE
Answer: "This coffee tastes like mud!"—"IT WAS JUST 'GROUND'"

92. **Jumbles:** AGONY GAMUT MASCOT POLISH
Answer: The hypochondriac said he was so sick he couldn't even do this—COMPLAIN

185

93. **Jumbles:** LEGAL EJECT JUNKET HOMING
Answer: He who laughs last probably doesn't this—GET THE JOKE

94. **Jumbles:** COVEY MANGE KIDNAP VIRTUE
Answer: He married her for her looks, but not this—THE KIND SHE OFTEN GAVE HIM

95. **Jumbles:** BANAL VAGUE FAUCET SHAKEN
Answer: What you can't make on a slow horse—A FAST BUCK

96. **Jumbles:** POUCH TARRY SECOND HICCUP
Answer: Another name for that reducing salon—THE "PAUNCH" SHOP

97. **Jumbles:** CRANK SHINY TIMELY FEWEST
Answer: Often dropped but seldom picked up—HINTS

98. **Jumbles:** AFOOT MAXIM VACANT SHANTY
Answer: What they called that wealthy playboy—"CASH-ANOVA"

99. **Jumbles:** SOGGY FRANC INCOME ATOMIC
Answer: It's hard to raise a child, especially when it's this—MORNING

100. **Jumbles:** BALKY OXIDE FABRIC PLENTY
Answer: A businessman is judged by the company he keeps…PROFITABLE

101. **Jumbles:** LILAC POWER MAGNET BUNKER
Answer: That bore won't stop talking until you start this—WALKING

102. **Jumbles:** GOING ROBIN TYPHUS PYTHON
Answer: How he usually ended a sentence—WITH A "PROPOSITION"

103. **Jumbles:** FORUM LOUSY ADMIRE JACKET
Answer: What he got when he bought that "stylish" raincoat—"SOAKED"

104. **Jumbles:** ASSAY CUBIC SAILOR CRAFTY
Answer: What she thought that new freshman was—VERY "FIRST-CLASS"

105. **Jumbles:** NUTTY BASIN FOSSIL LEGACY
Answer: What he got from the switchboard operator—THE BUSY SIGNAL

106. **Jumbles:** OBESE BALMY HAMMER THEORY
Answer: People with wanderlust seldom feel this—AT HOME AT HOME

107. **Jumbles:** GUESS AFTER KIDNAP ROBBER
Answer: The longer that sergeant stayed in the army—THE "RANKER" HE GOT

108. **Jumbles:** GLORY LINER DABBLE FORGET
Answer: What her attempts at cooking brought him—TO A BOIL

109. **Jumbles:** DELVE CARGO BUCKET LAYMAN
Answer: What was Michelangelo's favorite dessert?—MARBLE CAKE

110. **Jumbles:** FOYER PANDA BUSILY GAMBLE
Answer: How the sponge divers found their work—"ABSORBING"

111. **Jumbles:** PIKER ABBOT HOMAGE CLERGY
Answer: What lightning gave the Frankenstein monster—A BIG "CHARGE"

112. **Jumbles:** ERASE AWFUL FLAUNT CODGER
Answer: It's no "feat" to do this—DANCE ON FEET

113. **Jumbles:** GUEST FLAKE BANTER ELICIT
Answer: He drove as if he owned the road, which is why he ended up not owning this—A LICENSE

114. **Jumbles:** EXERT FUDGE MYSTIC STOLEN
Answer: What the egotist lets off plenty of—SELF-E"STEEM"

115. **Jumbles:** GROOM PHOTO AGHAST CLOVEN
Answer: What the bubble dancer said when he asked her to marry him—"NO SOAP"

116. **Jumbles:** AGONY LINER WATERY HOMAGE
Answer: Clothes make the man, especially when worn by this—THE RIGHT WOMAN

117. **Jumbles:** OUTDO AISLE BABOON TIPTOE
Answer: Never lend money to this guy!—A "DEBT" BEAT

118. **Jumbles:** UNCAP TRACT FRIGID IODINE
Answer: What many people start out on right after they return home from a vacation—AN EGO TRIP

119. **Jumbles:** GLAND FETID NIMBLE DROWSY
Answer: What a person who's always kicking seldom has—A LEG TO STAND ON

120. **Jumbles:** MOGUL JULEP BRIDGE COMMON
Answer: If a pedestrian is prone to be careless, he might end up this way—PRONE

121. **Jumbles:** FINIS ALIAS INFANT MISERY
Answer: What many an amateur gardener gets for his pains—LINIMENT

122. **Jumbles:** MANGY SUMAC DOUBLY GATHER
Answer: A man who is always asking for a loan is apt to be left this—ALONE

123. **Jumbles:** NOVEL DRAMA BYGONE SCHEME
Answer: Credit might be the means to live like this—BEYOND ONE'S MEANS

124. **Jumbles:** CATCH GOING VELVET BEWAIL
Answer: A date is something you must break when you this—HAVE TWO

125. **Jumbles:** HABIT PAPER RACIAL TURGID
Answer: A young person might improve his eyesight when he gets this—A HAIRCUT

126. **Jumbles:** ADULT GUESS CORNEA UNSOLD
Answer: What he said his wife's reasoning largely was—"SOUND"

127. **Jumbles:** SHEEP GLOVE STODGY HIDING
Answer: What his handicap in golf was—HIS HONESTY

128. **Jumbles:** METAL CRACK VARIED KETTLE
Answer: There was a lot of this in the waiting room of the employment agency—"IDLE" TALK

129. **Jumbles:** ADMIT FANCY DISMAL TRUDGE
Answer: What the lawyer who joined the nudist colony never had—A "SUIT" AGAIN

130. **Jumbles:** BLOOD EXACT MARTIN JAGUAR
Answer: A boxer who fails to carry out his second's suggestions is sometimes this—CARRIED OUT

131. **Jumbles:** SIXTY RABBI EASILY NEARLY
Answer: One is not at liberty to take this with others—LIBERTIES

132. **Jumbles:** NOISY REBEL MARAUD SQUALL
Answer: What the bodybuilder-turned–clam digger seemed to be—"MUSSEL"-BOUND

133. **Jumbles:** FANCY OFTEN NOZZLE RADIAL
Answer: What that tiresome speechmaker could not be after he was called on—CALLED OFF

134. **Jumbles:** DUCHY USURP BONNET MISUSE
Answer: His worst fault is telling other people—THEIRS

135. **Jumbles:** AGILE GRAVE BREACH FENNEL
Answer: What a brand-new father is about to enter into—A CHANGING WORLD

136. **Jumbles:** NATAL SILKY NUANCE DITHER
Answer: Used to open doors in the business world—HANDLES

137. **Jumbles:** ALTAR HOIST FLURRY PLAGUE
Answer: Why he was so popular in jail—HE WAS THE "LIFER" OF THE PARTY

138. **Jumbles:** EXUDE PARCH CORRAL FARINA
Answer: An outfit that makes one woman look slim often makes others look this—"'ROUND"

139. **Jumbles:** TEASE CHALK EXCISE DREDGE
Answer: That so-called comedian had them "in the aisles"…HEADED FOR THE EXITS

140. **Jumbles:** SHYLY ELDER MUFFLE AUTHOR
Answer: They said she was beautiful but not quite this—"ALL THERE"

141. **Jumbles:** KINKY GLEAM VALISE AWHILE
Answer: One way to keep friends is not to do this—
"GIVE THEM AWAY"

142. **Jumbles:** STAID POKER FENNEL TEAPOT
Answer: People who travel in order to become broadened sometimes return home this way—
"FLATTENED"

143. **Jumbles:** ODIUM WHOOP AGENCY CAMPER
Answer: What the first day of the week can be—
"MOAN" DAY

144. **Jumbles:** GOOSE ANKLE PARITY SAVAGE
Answer: What their babies' bedroom was called—
THE "NOISERY"

145. **Jumbles:** LINGO BOGUS GOLFER DRAGON
Answer: What they said when they saw the Grand Canyon—"GORGES"

146. **Jumbles:** LUSTY AGONY GYPSUM PRAYER
Answer: Keeping up with the Joneses might also involve keeping up with these—THE PAYMENTS

147. **Jumbles:** BROOK GROOM SUNDAE CIPHER
Answer: What those society "crumbs" were held together by—"DOUGH"

148. **Jumbles:** SHINY EJECT RUBBER MIDDAY
Answer: What the billionaire left when he died—
MUCH TO BE DESIRED

149. **Jumbles:** IRONY ADMIT FOMENT DOUBLE
Answer: Permissive parents don't mind when their kids this—DON'T MIND

150. **Jumbles:** COCOA OUTDO BUTTER ZENITH
Answer: He doesn't like to be ordered around unless it's this—A ROUND OF BOOZE

151. **Jumbles:** RIGOR GAMUT SOLACE RATION
Answer: What she wished her admirers would practice—"ARMS" CONTROL

152. **Jumbles:** GRIMY ERUPT FEUDAL JESTER
Answer: What an unethical trustee sometimes ends up as—A TRUSTY

153. **Jumbles:** AWFUL PAPER JETSAM HINDER
Answer: What nepotism means in the field of employment—TO PUT ON "HEIRS"

154. **Jumbles:** MURKY WHILE JACKAL RAMROD
Answer: A four-letter word that some people find most "objectionable"—"WORK"

155. **Jumbles:** TOXIN KAPOK CAUGHT GRIMLY
Answer: Sometimes when the players do the running, the fans do this—THE KICKING

156. **Jumbles:** BASIS ENACT RABBIT AFLOAT
Answer: What some parents experience when they have teenage kids—"EARITATION"

157. **Jumbles:** DALLY VERVE EIGHTY BEATEN
Answer: What many family problems are—
ALL "RELATIVE"

158. **Jumbles:** HONEY LARVA WALNUT MORBID
Answer: If he starts right out complaining about her cooking, she'll learn better…OR HE WILL

159. **Jumbles:** PIETY RAPID UNPAID STYLUS
Answer: How many a "checkered" career ends up—
IN A STRIPED SUIT

160. **Jumbles:** SURLY PHONY JUSTLY FALTER
Answer: Any man who survives by "doing nothing" is probably really doing this—OTHERS

161. **Jumbles:** KITTEN HAIRDO PURITY LAVISH SCROLL HANSOM
Answer: When the carpenters got together, they had a—PANEL DISCUSSION

162. **Jumbles:** TRYING WOEFUL VACANT INTENT BEDBUG LAXITY
Answer: What the submarine crew did on shore leave—
WENT INTO A DIVE

163. **Jumbles:** PAUPER ALWAYS AUTHOR RANCID ZEALOT HELIUM
Answer: When the nurse went over budget, her credit cards became this—A WEALTH HAZARD

164. **Jumbles:** SNUGLY LANCER BAKING OBLIGE SWERVE INJURY
Answer: Mom was greeted with this when she came home—"BREAKING" NEWS

165. **Jumbles:** KNOTTY ENGULF NORMAL GALAXY JUNIOR IMMUNE
Answer: What the instruction book gave the plumber's apprentice—"MANUAL" TRAINING

166. **Jumbles:** GUZZLE VENDOR BELLOW LACKEY FAMISH NEEDLE
Answer: Another name for bridesmaids in the old South—WEDDING BELLES

167. **Jumbles:** MANAGE BYWORD DIVERT BEHIND SUGARY SPONGE
Answer: What Mom gave Junior when she saw his outfit—A DRESSING DOWN

168. **Jumbles:** INTONE MYOPIC FITFUL DAMASK OUTFIT BRONCO
Answer: Needed to get the hay in the barn—
A "LOFT-Y" AMBITION

169. **Jumbles:** CONVEX ASSURE PALATE LIMPID SADIST TUSSLE
Answer: How blue-blood matrons know who is who—
"SOCIAL" STUDIES

170. **Jumbles:** MUSEUM QUENCH RAVAGE DECODE UNEASY PENCIL
Answer: What the magician looked for in his contract—
AN "ESCAPE" CLAUSE

171. **Jumbles:** STURDY POLICY HUNGRY EROTIC CAMPER PRIMED
Answer: A successful vegetable farmer will do this—
PRODUCE PRODUCE

172. **Jumbles:** UNIQUE PENMAN MARKUP EMBARK DEPICT EQUITY
Answer: What the climber experienced when he couldn't reach the summit—A PEAK PEEK PIQUE

173. **Jumbles:** CORNER WEASEL ABRUPT PURIFY KINGLY GRASSY
Answer: What the doctor resorted to when the credit charges got too high—"PLASTIC" SURGERY

174. **Jumbles:** LAWFUL UNLOCK TUXEDO BOBBIN GOPHER PARLOR
Answer: The tailor had trouble with the wrestler because he was—TOUGH TO PIN DOWN

175. **Jumbles:** BECALM MORGUE AWHILE FRACAS PILLAR BEGONE
Answer: The ventriloquist said his dummy was this—
A FIGURE OF "SPEECH"

176. **Jumbles:** BUTTON IMBUED RENEGE MYRIAD SHERRY MARLIN
Answer: The office worker yearned for a day at the beach because she had—A "BURNING" DESIRE

177. **Jumbles:** BENUMB UNTRUE ZENITH MEMOIR LEGUME STODGY
Answer: How did the tailors settle their differences?—
"IRONED" THEM OUT

178. **Jumbles:** HOMAGE LARYNX GRATIS PAUNCH BELIEF MILDEW
Answer: What Mom became when she polished the silverware—A SHINING EXAMPLE

179. **Jumbles:** EMPLOY OXYGEN PRISON TROUGH COMPEL FILLET
Answer: When his prose brought tears to her eyes, she said it was—POETRY EMOTION

180. **Jumbles:** NIMBLE ITALIC ENMITY DEMISE SULTRY ENTICE
Answer: What the psychiatrist faced when he was stopped for speeding—AN IDENTITY CRISIS

Need More Jumbles®?

Order any of these books through your bookseller or call Triumph Books toll-free at 800-335-5323.

Jumble® Books

More than 175 puzzles each!

Cowboy Jumble®
ISBN: 978-1-62937-355-3

Jammin' Jumble®
ISBN: 1-57243-844-4

Java Jumble®
ISBN: 978-1-60078-415-6

Jazzy Jumble®
ISBN: 978-1-57243-962-7

Jet Set Jumble®
ISBN: 978-1-60078-353-1

Joyful Jumble®
ISBN: 978-1-60078-079-0

Juke Joint Jumble®
ISBN: 978-1-60078-295-4

Jumble® Anniversary
ISBN: 987-1-62937-734-6

Jumble® at Work
ISBN: 1-57243-147-4

Jumble® Ballet
ISBN: 978-1-62937-616-5

Jumble® Birthday
ISBN: 978-1-62937-652-3

Jumble® Celebration
ISBN: 978-1-60078-134-6

Jumble® Circus
ISBN: 978-1-60078-739-3

Jumble® Cuisine
ISBN: 978-1-62937-735-3

Jumble® Drag Race
ISBN: 978-1-62937-483-3

Jumble® Ever After
ISBN: 978-1-62937-785-8

Jumble® Explorer
ISBN: 978-1-60078-854-3

Jumble® Explosion
ISBN: 978-1-60078-078-3

Jumble® Fever
ISBN: 1-57243-593-3

Jumble® Fiesta
ISBN: 1-57243-626-3

Jumble® Fun
ISBN: 1-57243-379-5

Jumble® Galaxy
ISBN: 978-1-60078-583-2

Jumble® Garden
ISBN: 978-1-62937-653-0

Jumble® Genius
ISBN: 1-57243-896-7

Jumble® Geography
ISBN: 978-1-62937-615-8

Jumble® Getaway
ISBN: 978-1-60078-547-4

Jumble® Gold
ISBN: 978-1-62937-354-6

Jumble® Grab Bag
ISBN: 1-57243-273-X

Jumble® Gymnastics
ISBN: 978-1-62937-306-5

Jumble® Jackpot
ISBN: 1-57243-897-5

Jumble® Jailbreak
ISBN: 978-1-62937-002-6

Jumble® Jambalaya
ISBN: 978-1-60078-294-7

Jumble® Jamboree
ISBN: 1-57243-696-4

Jumble® Jitterbug
ISBN: 978-1-60078-584-9

Jumble® Journey
ISBN: 978-1-62937-549-6

Jumble® Jubilation
ISBN: 978-1-62937-784-1

Jumble® Jubilee
ISBN: 1-57243-231-4

Jumble® Juggernaut
ISBN: 978-1-60078-026-4

Jumble® Junction
ISBN: 1-57243-380-9

Jumble® Jungle
ISBN: 978-1-57243-961-0

Jumble® Kingdom
ISBN: 978-1-62937-079-8

Jumble® Knockout
ISBN: 978-1-62937-078-1

Jumble® Madness
ISBN: 1-892049-24-4

Jumble® Magic
ISBN: 978-1-60078-795-9

Jumble® Marathon
ISBN: 978-1-60078-944-1

Jumble® Neighbor
ISBN: 978-1-62937-845-9

Jumble® Parachute
ISBN: 978-1-62937-548-9

Jumble® Safari
ISBN: 978-1-60078-675-4

Jumble® See & Search
ISBN: 1-57243-549-6

Jumble® See & Search 2
ISBN: 1-57243-734-0

Jumble® Sensation
ISBN: 978-1-60078-548-1

Jumble® Surprise
ISBN: 1-57243-320-5

Jumble® Symphony
ISBN: 978-1-62937-131-3

Jumble® Theater
ISBN: 978-1-62937-484-03

Jumble® University
ISBN: 978-1-62937-001-9

Jumble® Unleashed
ISBN: 978-1-62937-844-2

Jumble® Vacation
ISBN: 978-1-60078-796-6

Jumble® Wedding
ISBN: 978-1-62937-307-2

Jumble® Workout
ISBN: 978-1-60078-943-4

Jumpin' Jumble®
ISBN: 978-1-60078-027-1

Lunar Jumble®
ISBN: 978-1-60078-853-6

Monster Jumble®
ISBN: 978-1-62937-213-6

Mystic Jumble®
ISBN: 978-1-62937-130-6

Outer Space Jumble®
ISBN: 978-1-60078-416-3

Rainy Day Jumble®
ISBN: 978-1-60078-352-4

Ready, Set, Jumble®
ISBN: 978-1-60078-133-0

Rock 'n' Roll Jumble®
ISBN: 978-1-60078-674-7

Royal Jumble®
ISBN: 978-1-60078-738-6

Sports Jumble®
ISBN: 1-57243-113-X

Summer Fun Jumble®
ISBN: 1-57243-114-8

Touchdown Jumble®
ISBN: 978-1-62937-212-9

Travel Jumble®
ISBN: 1-57243-198-9

TV Jumble®
ISBN: 1-57243-461-9

Oversize Jumble® Books

More than 500 puzzles each!

Generous Jumble®
ISBN: 1-57243-385-X

Giant Jumble®
ISBN: 1-57243-349-3

Gigantic Jumble®
ISBN: 1-57243-426-0

Jumbo Jumble®
ISBN: 1-57243-314-0

The Very Best of Jumble® BrainBusters
ISBN: 1-57243-845-2

Jumble® Crosswords™

More than 175 puzzles each!

More Jumble® Crosswords™
ISBN: 1-57243-386-8

Jumble® Crosswords™ Jackpot
ISBN: 1-57243-615-8

Jumble® Crosswords™ Jamboree
ISBN: 1-57243-787-1

Jumble® BrainBusters™

More than 175 puzzles each!

Jumble® BrainBusters™
ISBN: 1-892049-28-7

Jumble® BrainBusters™ II
ISBN: 1-57243-424-4

Jumble® BrainBusters™ III
ISBN: 1-57243-463-5

Jumble® BrainBusters™ IV
ISBN: 1-57243-489-9

Jumble® BrainBusters™ 5
ISBN: 1-57243-548-8

Jumble® BrainBusters™ Bonanza
ISBN: 1-57243-616-6

Boggle™ BrainBusters™
ISBN: 1-57243-592-5

Boggle™ BrainBusters™ 2
ISBN: 1-57243-788-X

Jumble® BrainBusters™ Junior
ISBN: 1-892049-29-5

Jumble® BrainBusters™ Junior II
ISBN: 1-57243-425-2

Fun in the Sun with Jumble® BrainBusters™
ISBN: 1-57243-733-2